WINE

WINE

*everything you ever
wanted to know about*

RED, WHITE,
ROSÉ
& FIZZ

Jane Parkinson

with photography by Toby Scott

RYLAND PETERS & SMALL
LONDON • NEW YORK

Designers Paul Stradling, Manisha Patel and Emily Breen
Commissioning Editor Stephanie Milner
Production David Hearn
Picture Researcher Christina Borsi
Art Director Leslie Harrington
Editorial Director Julia Charles
Publisher Cindy Richards

Photographer Toby Scott
Photographer's Assistant Benjamin Wisely
Prop Stylist Luis Peral
Food Stylist Rosie Reynolds

This abridged edition published in 2019
First published in 2014
by Ryland Peters & Small,
20–21 Jockey's Fields,
London WC1R 4BW
and
341 E 116th St
New York NY 10029

www.rylandpeters.com

Text copyright © Jane Parkinson 2014,
2017, 2019
Design and commissioned photographs
copyright © Ryland Peters & Small 2014,
2017, 2019 (see page 207 for other credits)

ISBN: 978-1-78879-076-5

Printed and bound in China

10 9 8 7 6 5 4 3 2 1

A CIP record for this book is available from
the British Library.
US Library of Congress cataloging-in-
publication data has been applied for.

CONTENTS

INTRODUCTION

Feeling thirsty but not sure what to drink? Then this is the book for you. I love being asked what wines people should try, it's one of the favourite parts of my job. From my personal favourites to fashionable wines or the bottles that offer the best value, I hope I answer everyone's questions (and more) here in this book, which is my go-to guide for those that are curious about wine and love all the flavours that come with it. With that in mind, I chat through all the topics in my kind of everyday language. This means there isn't much jargon to be found, but when it does make the odd appearance, I promise an explanation quickly follows.

The way we buy, serve, enjoy and match wine has changed massively in the last couple of decades, partly because we've never been so spoilt for choice. And so, in this book, I introduce you to glorious grape varieties, some known and perhaps some lesser-known, but in each case I explain where they are grown, how the wine should taste and why, for example, it might be blended with another grape. Occasionally, I also namedrop a particularly good producer because I am also constantly asked for these recommendations too.

In The Bar, I take a closer look at serving wine, whether it's the trends in glass shapes, nifty serving paraphernalia or serving temperatures. All of this might seem a bit old school to some people, but they can play a really important role in affecting how a wine will taste so if you want to make the most of your wine make sure you take a peek.

You'll also see that this book is peppered with various ad hoc wine topics, the kind that come up often but no one ever seems to get a definitive answer to. They range from why it's good to chill red wine to the difference between organic, biodynamic and natural wine, so I hope you find these topics useful along the way.

No matter where you are on your wine journey, if you're interested in delving more into the world of wine, then this book should give you extra insight into what is happening all around us, and who is doing what, where, and hopefully, well.

Happy drinking.

SETTING THE WINE SCENE

Knowing the name of the grape inside a bottle has completely changed the face of wine and how we drink it. Before my time and possibly yours, too, wine names like Chablis, Bordeaux, Sancerre, Rioja and Chianti were flung about with such carefree ease it gave wine completely the wrong image. That was turned on its head about 25–30 years ago, largely by people in the southern hemisphere and North America; places we call the New World. These guys started to make serious wine and had the confidence to slap the grape variety boldly on the front of a bottle. This change to labelling wine opened the floodgates for wine appreciation. Wine became exciting, aspirational and easier to understand. Fast-track to today, and now there's just as much (if not more) global interest in the names Chardonnay, Cabernet Sauvignon, Merlot, Sauvignon Blanc, Tempranillo, or even Sangiovese, as there ever was in the Old World names of the regions in which these grape varieties were – and still are – made.

THE NEW OLD WORLD

It's great news for us that countries like Italy, Spain, France and Portugal have raised their game in the face of stiff competition from New World winemakers. These countries are blessed with high-quality local grape varieties, each suited to its own special environment; and together with a general improvement in technology the world over, there's an endless source of delicious European wines now at our fingertips. For more gorgeous European wines Flagship reds (see pages 76–81), Italian whites (see pages 134–137) and Spanish whites (see pages 138–143).

FRANCE

The tiny Jura region is now a haven of delicious characterful white wines made with local grapes Chardonnay and Savagnin with a nutty, salty flavour that's gorgeously unique and moreish.

While the Jura is doing a great job with white wines it is also making hedonistically beautiful light, bright and sappy red wines from local grapes Pinot Noir, Trousseau and Poulsard.

ITALY

All across the north of the country, from Piedmont to Friuli, Italy is a melting pot of zingy and refreshing whites made from local grapes with personality and attitude, such as floral Arneis, zesty Friulano or the appley Ribolla Gialla.

The days of southern Italy churning out masses of bulk red wine are changing. Instead, carefully crafted, inky-dark, spicy reds are being made from local grapes, such as the dark and brooding Aglianico in Campania, or the meaty grape Negroamaro from Puglia, or the peppery Nerello Mascalese from Sicily.

SPAIN

Although Albariño is delicious and perfect with seafood, look out for crisp and fruity white wines made from Verdejo in Rueda, Godello in Valdeorras and the modern take on white Rioja, which is less oaky.

In north-west Spain, a local grape called Mencía has come of age in the region of Bierzo. It's full of black fruits with a spicy flavour – as is another Spanish grape, Monastrell. Both are great alternatives if you're stuck in a red Rioja rut.

PORTUGAL

Vinho Verde is more than just retro-cool; it makes some seriously delicious white wines. The Loureiro grape used here is floral while Alvarinho is richer, and these are the two grapes worth looking out for. The Douro Valley is also a haven for pretty, citrus-fresh white wines made from local grapes.

Speaking of the Douro Valley, it's also making terrific red wines from the same grape varieties you'd find in the region's most famous wine, Port. I'm talking about Touriga Nacional and Tinta Roriz (Tempranillo). These table reds have a very pure blackberry character with lovely, dry spice flavours of cumin and cinnamon.

AUSTRIA
Blaufränkisch *Say it: blauw-fran-kish*
This local Austrian red grape varies from very light (in a Beaujolais style) to rich and spicy. I think it's especially tasty when it's lighter and quaffable.

THE NEW NEW WORLD
As the New World wine countries evolve, they're branching out from the wines and grapes that initially made them famous. This evolution is happening because, as the regions age, the locals have a better understanding of their land's potential with other grapes, plus they're determined to prove to the world they can perfect more than just one style or grape!

AUSTRALIA
Australians are now using 'other' European grapes partly to boost their sophistication credentials. In warmer regions like McLaren Vale, you'll find varieties such as Sicily's Nero d'Avola and Spain's Tempranillo, while the Adelaide Hills region makes Austria's Grüner Veltliner well.

NEW ZEALAND
New Zealand is working hard to show it's more than a one-trick (Sauvignon Blanc) or even two-trick (Pinot Noir) pony. With red wine, Syrah/Shiraz is the most exciting grape, especially in Waiheke Island and Hawke's Bay. Meanwhile, many regions are making fantastic Chardonnay and Riesling.

CHINA
Let's wait and see, but China continues its drive to be a wine force to be reckoned with. Grenache is playing its part – apparently lots is being planted. Watch this space.

USA (CALIFORNIA)

One of the most exciting and fast-changing wine scenes these days is California. In the cooler north of Sonoma, elegant cool climate wines, such as Chardonnay, Pinot Noir and Syrah, are gaining a serious reputation, especially from excellent smaller producers like Arnot-Roberts, but in truth there are gems popping up all over the place from Monterey to Santa Barbara.

SOUTH AFRICA

A collaborative force of young gun producers with skill and high standards has made South Africa a must-watch country for white and red wines these days. Initially coming out of the Swartland region but now spanning the country, these producers are making astonishing wines from Chenin Blanc, Chardonnay, Syrah, Pinot Noir and Cinsault.

Blends

Originally, New World wines traded on their easy-to-understand credentials. This included championing wines made from a single grape variety (varietal wines), which was proudly splashed across the wine bottle's front label. This pushed grape varieties into the limelight, but no one, not even the New World guys, ever claimed these varietal wines were superior to blended wines, and yet the world started to think they were. Some of the most prized, expensive and serious wines in the world are actually blends, so don't dismiss them.

Label logic

The labels on New World wine bottles lead with grape variety, and we love this easy way of telling us exactly what's inside the bottle. In fact, it's so popular that Old World countries have started tweaking their labelling laws to (sometimes) allow grape varieties on their labels as well.

France: Know your crus

'Cru' translates as 'growth' in English, and the quality categories of Grand and Premier Cru are used in the French wine regions of Burgundy and Alsace, but also in Champagne, albeit in a different way. Although each region has its own little quirks about what determines the level of cru, Grand Cru is always top dog, followed by Premier Cru. Eating out? On wine lists, you'll commonly see Grand Cru shortened to 'GC', and Premier Cru shortened to 'PC' or '1er Cru'.

Bordeaux: Classifications

One part of the Bordeaux region is called the Médoc, and this is where Cabernet Sauvignon reigns supreme. Sometimes, the Médoc is called 'the Left Bank', in relation to the rivers Gironde and Garonne. The Left Bank of Bordeaux has a châteaux hierarchy that was created in 1855, and it still exists today. The '1855 classification', as it is known, ranks Bordeaux châteaux and there are five levels. At the pinnacle are the esteemed and pricey First Growths, with only five châteaux in this top tier. On Bordeaux's Right Bank, Merlot reigns supreme, and this is where you find the village of St-Emilion, which also has its own classification system. The most prestigious of these is Premier Grand Cru Classé, which is sub-divided again into two tiers, A and B. Then comes Grand Cru Classé.

Italy: To riserva or non-riserva

'Riserva' usually indicates a producer's higher-quality wine – a wine that has been aged for a longer period than non-riserva wines. It can also mean higher alcohol.

Germany: Name by name

Still plagued by the sweetness tag; if you want to know the style of German Riesling, look out for these labels:

KABINETT *Say it: ka-been-et* Dry wine

SPÄTLESE *Say it: shpate-lay-zer* Dry or slightly sweet wine

AUSLESE *Say it: owz-lay-zer* Sweet-ish wine

BEERENAUSLESE (BA) *Say it: bear-ein-owz-lay-zer* Sweet wine

TROCKENBEERENAUSLESE (TBA) *Say it: trok-en-bear-ein-owz-lay-zer* Even sweeter wine

EISWEIN *Say it: ice-vine* Super-sweet wine

Spain: Rank your reserva

Spanish red wines are often labelled by reserva. Each indicates an ageing period, some of which is in oak:

GRAN RESERVA Aged for a minimum of 5 years

RESERVA RED WINES Aged for a minimum of 3 years

RESERVA WHITE WINES Aged for a minimum of 2 years

Good label innovations

1. QR codes or those little tags you can rip off a bottle's back label. Both of these help you to remember the name of a wine you've drunk while out and about.

2. The Riesling sweetness scale. Riesling continues to have an identity crisis because people are wary of it being too sweet. This label is a universal scale printed on the back of bottles.

RED

Reds are now as diverse as they are delicious. From cosy and comforting to beefy and spicy to delicate and fragrant, today's red wine scene champions the full spectrum of styles available and not just the ones that shout the loudest with their fruit, spice or tannin, much of which is down to the choice of raw material – the grape.

PINOT NOIR

CHARACTERISTICS
earthy • elegant • fresh • hedonistic • juicy • perfumed • smooth • succulent

SMELLS
herbaceous • perfumed • smoky toasty

TASTES OF
beetroot/beet • cranberry • mushroom • plum pomegranate • raspberry • red • cherry • rhubarb • strawberry • truffle vanilla

The diva of wine grapes, Pinot Noir is fussy about where it's grown, and that can push up its price. But when it's happy and made well, it's the ultimate in wine hedonism. Pinot Noir usually grows best in cooler climates and produces a pale liquid by red wine standards. It's lovely when young and full of juicy strawberry and red cherry flavours, but it's also delicious when older, tasting smooth and earthy.

Pinot Noir's home is Burgundy, and winemakers around the world are mesmerized and inspired by the beautiful wine that Pinot Noir makes in this region. Producers everywhere, though, have to be careful not to slather the grape in too much oak or let the alcohol level creep too high because both can spoil this grape's trademark delicacy. Some people refer to Pinot Noir simply as 'Pinot'. You can do this, too, but tread carefully, as there are plenty of other grapes in the Pinot family, like Pinot Gris and Pinot Blanc.

Pinot Noir is also a vital ingredient in some of the world's best sparkling wines. The pulp of the grape (where the juice comes from) is quickly removed from the skins after harvest so the wine doesn't take on any pink colour from the skins, unless you want a rosé. A fizz made entirely from Pinot Noir will often be given the name Blanc de Noirs, roughly translated as white wine made from black grapes. It also makes great pink fizz, and is done one of two ways. The first is to add some red Pinot Noir wine to white Champagne, the other is to let the skin of the grape stay in contact with the wine for enough time to let the colour seep into the wine. This is called *saignée* (bleeding).

REGIONS & FLAVOURS

HOME REGION BURGUNDY, FRANCE

Red Burgundy is made from Pinot Noir. That's the easy bit. Napoleonic laws of heritance, based on inheritance by bloodline, have meant that growers' vineyards have been hugely fragmented over the years. One small plot could be shared by 90 growers, all producing wines that are rare, and this contributes to their higher-than-average price. The most revered strip of vineyards in Burgundy is split in two. The southern half, Côte de Beaune, is more Chardonnay territory, but you can still find elegant Pinot Noirs there. The northern half, Côte de Nuits, is Pinot Noir country. The wines here are usually a bit richer than in the south, with a savoury, earthy character as well as plump fruit.

ITALY

Pinot Nero, as it is called locally, thrives in the cool Italian north, near the Alps. Especially so in Alto Adige, where it makes fresh wines with bright cherry flavours. It's also made in Lombardy, where it is essential to the production of the sparkling wine Franciacorta (see pages 172–175).

Labelling red Burgundy

In descending order of prestige, red Burgundy (always made from Pinot Noir) is labelled: Grand Cru; Premier Cru; (The name of a village), for example Pommard; (The name of a group of villages), for example Côte de Nuits-Villages; Bourgogne.

GERMANY

Spätburgunder, as it's known locally, is becoming increasingly important in Germany. There's a lot more of it around now than there was even 15 years ago, and it's more popular in the South, in regions like Baden and Pfalz, where it's warm enough to ripen properly. These wines are delicate, and come from vines on schist-based soils that give a stony, slate-like flavour to them. In other words, they're usually savoury styles of Pinot Noir, rather than those that are full of juicy fruit. They're hugely underestimated, very classy, and they're becoming a must-try style of Pinot.

USA

There are a few great little pockets of Pinot Noir expertise in the United States. In California, Russian River Valley and Los Carneros do a delicious job. Californian Pinot Noir is usually bigger and fruitier in style than many other Pinot Noir-producing regions, and Los Carneros makes excellent sparkling wines as well as red Pinot Noir. In Oregon, Pinot Noir is the flagship grape, and the Oregon sub-region of Willamette Valley excels in making it. Here, the wines are elegant and perfumed, and those I really enjoy come from Domaine Drouhin, Bergstrom and Cristom.

CHILE

Chile produces real value-for-money, young and juicy Pinot Noir, especially from the now-renowned regions of Casablanca and San Antonio. The sophistication of its Pinot Noirs is growing all the time, especially when made from grapes from cooler, newish spots like Leyda and Paradones. Cono Sur makes many levels of Pinot Noir and the range is always consistently good. Viña Mar was one of the Chilean Pinot Noir pioneers and still makes great Pinots today. Casa Real also makes fantastic wine in Paradones, while Viña Leyda makes fresh, coastal Pinot Noir that is fruity but with a distinct salty kick.

NEW ZEALAND

The cool, maritime New Zealand climate is great for Pinot Noir and, a bit like Chardonnay, it is made consistently well in lots of regions. Historically, Martinborough was the region with the best reputation, and it still makes excellent Pinot Noirs from producers like Ata Rangi and Craggy Range.

However, the region that makes the biggest splash with top-end NZ Pinot Noir these days is Central Otago. This is the most southerly wine-producing region in the world. It makes achingly beautiful Pinot Noir, and is destined for even greater things in years to come. The wines are dense in cherry fruit flavours, with a gentle, toasty richness and delicate spice; it's really serious stuff. There's an iconic producer here, in Felton Road, and while these wines are delicious, other producers I like very much include Mount Edward, Rippon, Doctors Flat and Burn Cottage.

Marlborough also makes delicious Pinot Noir with raspberry and cherry fruit, and a delicate savoury character as well. Some of the most serious (and gorgeous!) I know are from Dog Point and Seresin.

EASTERN EUROPE

Sounds crazy? Perhaps. But there's no denying that Bulgaria, Romania and Hungary are places to watch for good-value Pinot Noir. And, although they're on-the-up in terms of easy-drinking and light Pinot Noirs, these countries haven't shown any signs of competing with complex Pinot Noir-producing regions. Yet. The best I have tasted so far comes from Bulgaria and a producer called Edoardo Miroglio.

THE REST OF FRANCE

Let's not forget the Loire Valley for Pinot Noir. Red Sancerre, especially, makes gorgeous Pinot Noirs to drink in spring and summer. They're vibrant, perky and fresh. I especially like those from Vincent Delaporte and Gérard et Pierre Morin.

Alsace, which has a pretty cool climate, makes a similarly savoury style of Pinot Noir to those from Baden in Germany, which is just across the border. And even though it's much warmer, we're now seeing ripe and juicy Pinot Noir coming from the south of France, although it's not a natural home for it, and at the moment, that warmth shows in the wines.

AUSTRALIA

Pockets of Australia are now making some world-class Pinot Noir, and much of it is found in the states of Tasmania and Victoria where cooler temperatures play to this grape's fussy demands. In Victoria's Yarra Valley, excellent Pinots being made by Mac Forbes, Timo Mayer and Gembrook Hill, while in Mornington Peninsula there's a whole host of top-notch Pinot producers, including Paringa Estate and Yabby Lake.

SOUTH AFRICA

The planting of Pinot Noir here is mostly for sparkling wine production, but even so there has been a rise in quantity and quality of red Pinot Noir made here, too. The Hemel-en-Aarde region with its cool ocean breezes is often though of as the best for Pinot Noir and it's where producers like Crystallum make stunning wines, Elgin is also doing great things, as Cathy Marshall is proving, but there are also delicious ones in the country's most famous region Stellenbosch, such as those made by Craven.

Chill down

If you're serving Pinot Noir with fish, or as a lighter summer wine, don't be afraid to chill it for 15 minutes in the fridge. The bright fruit will taste extra-fresh with a touch of chill to it. See page 32 for more information.

Clos St Louis vineyard, Fixin, Côte de Nuits, Burgundy, France

SYRAH/SHIRAZ

CHARACTERISTICS
elegant • meaty •
peppery •
perfumed • rich •
smoky • spicy

SMELLS
herbaceous • oaky
smoky • toasty

TASTES OF
aniseed • bacon •
blackberry •
blackcurrant •
black olive •
black pepper •
cherry • chocolate
coffee • currants •
eucalyptus •
fruit cake • jam/
jelly • nuts • plum •
raspberry •
rosemary • thyme

Want to know how a Syrah or Shiraz is going to taste? Just look at its name. Syrah used to be the name exclusively used for this grape in the Old World, while the New World favoured Shiraz. Now, winemakers in the New World often think their wines have the panache and style of the Old World Syrahs, so now they're also starting to call their wines Syrah instead of Shiraz. This means that the name on the label gives an indication of the style of Syrah/Shiraz it's going to be. Shiraz in its classic form is big and ballsy, jammed with black fruits, but then also crammed with a hit of black pepper, spice and liquorice. Syrah, on the other hand, is a more genteel affair. It still has plenty of black fruit, but it's often tamed with a mushroom-flavoured earthy character.

Syrah/Shiraz is just as tasty when it's made on its own as it is when it's blended with other grapes in a wine. Some of its favourite blending partners are Grenache and Mourvèdre, but you can also find it blended with Cabernet Sauvignon. And then one of its classic blending partners is actually Viognier, a white grape. Classy, flavoursome, versatile; that's Syrah/Shiraz.

REGIONS & FLAVOURS

HOME REGION RHÔNE VALLEY, FRANCE

The east strip of France that runs southwards from Lyon to Avignon
is a Mecca for Syrah. In wine terms, the Rhône is split in two: north
and south. In the north, Lyon to Montélimar, Syrah is the only red
grape allowed, although it's often blended with the white Viognier
grape here. In the south, Syrah is blended with a fanfare of other
grapes, such as Grenache, Mourvèdre and Cinsault. Famous wine
regions and styles here, such as Gigondas and Châteauneuf-du-Pape,
are usually made from Syrah blends. These wines are big and bold,
and can be quite tannic when young, but the good ones can age for
many years. A classic aroma and taste description for these particular
Syrahs is smoky bacon.

AUSTRALIA

Most Australians opt for the name Shiraz, and although a quality can
range from basic to mind-blowingly good, I think it's been victim of its
own success. While the blockbuster-spicy, fruit-bomb Shiraz took the
world by storm in the late 1990s, most people now (wrongly) assume
that all Australian Shiraz is too big to handle. This definitely isn't the
case. So give it another go, please! The region that's really held up on
a pedestal for its Shiraz is Barossa Valley, in South Australia. These
wines can command an eye-watering price but they're often worth it.
Because it is the signature red grape, Shiraz is popular all over
Australia, although the overworked, soupy, over-alcoholic versions

The lowdown on Syrah / Shiraz

A red grape with a pedigree, originally from the Rhône Valley in
France, it's just as easy to find this blended with other grapes as a
single-grape variety. It can be drunk when young, but high-quality
styles also age well.

that made it notorious are far less common now. Essentially, Australian Shiraz comes down to this: lovely, ripe blackcurrant fruit, a lick of spice and liquorice with a hit of eucalyptus. Look to Barossa for polished panache, McLaren Vale for punchy power, and Victoria for genteel elegance. Some of my favourite Australian Shiraz producers are Clonakilla, Henshke, Jasper Hill and Luke Lambert.

SOUTH AFRICA

South Africa is now hot property for Syrah/Shiraz and its constant improvement in quality has really helped to raise the reputation of this country's red wine scene, one that has previously been slighted by red wines with a burnt-rubber aroma and flavour (that problem seems to be much less widespread these days). Of all the countries that name the wines Syrah/Shiraz, perhaps South Africa is the most split when it comes to choosing what to call it. The most exciting South African region for Syrah at the moment is Swartland, just north of Cape Town, where all (okay, many of) the hip, cool, up-and-coming winemakers are making some seriously sophisticated wines, although Stellenbosch still has its fair share of great producers, too. The good ones have a purity and lusciousness to the fruit, with lots of dark/bittersweet chocolate flavours: big, ripe and juicy. Some of my favourite producers are Mullineux and Craven.

CHILE

Chilean Syrah/Shiraz is important for Chile's high-quality wine scene. And even though it's work in progress, the newly discovered regions in northern Chile are really helping Syrah/Shiraz's cause, especially in the Elqui Valley, where Syrah/Shiraz is the signature grape. These wines are pure in black fruit with a cool, black-pepper edge. Pretty classy stuff for a region that's still so new. Only a handful of producers exist, but my tip for now is to try the wines of Viña Falernia.

NEW ZEALAND

This is Syrah/Shiraz with a cool-climate twist, and is, like in Chile, still not produced in huge quantities, but when it's made here, it's usually very good. I like the reserved style, with the crushed black-pepper spice that the cooler temperature brings to the flesh of the wine. Hawkes Bay and Waiheke Island are making awesome Syrah/Shiraz styles. Try Trinity Hill and The Hay Paddock.

CALIFORNIA

The view that Syrah/Shiraz should be some dense chewy fruit bomb has changed in California in recent years and now a new wave of producers are really honing in on Syrah's elegance and spicy qualities, such as Arnot-Roberts and Wind Gap in the cooler climes of Sonoma.

Vineyard in Barossa Valley, South Australia

Chilling red wine

Here's the thing: chilling red wine isn't done anywhere near enough. Over the years we've been conditioned into thinking red wines need to be served at room temperature, but this is a modern-day fallacy because this advice was dished out in the time of pre-central heating, when rooms were generally a lot cooler. Which means that very few red wines taste their best at today's version of room temperature. Plus, some grape varieties show even better when the wines taste fresher and spicier, and this is easily achieved by chilling a red wine. Not everyone wants their wine to taste that way, I get that, but it can be a really lovely way to drink red wine, especially in the summer. The best 'chill-able' red wines have low tannin and low alcohol.

Reds you can serve straight from the fridge:
BEAUJOLAIS & BEAUJOLAIS NOUVEAU (MADE WITH GAMAY)
These are the two most basic levels of Beaujolais. Beaujolais Nouveau is sold in November each year as a very young wine and is super-fruity.
LAMBRUSCO A slightly sparkling Italian wine that's brilliant with pizza.

Reds you can serve 15 minutes after leaving the fridge:
BEAUJOLAIS-VILLAGES & BEAUJOLAIS CRU (MADE WITH GAMAY)
Cru is the highest quality category of Beaujolais, which is less fruity than cheaper Beaujolais, but still fruity enough to be chilled happily.
PINOT NOIR Choose lighter styles of Pinot Noir from cooler places, when they're fruity and unoaked.
CABERNET FRANC Famous for its green herbal aroma, this grape often tastes best when served cool. Those from the Loire Valley are especially good.
ZWEIGELT *Say it: Sv-eye-gelt* Austria's lightest and perkiest red grape loves having a chilly edge to it.

FRAPPATO A very juicy, light and jammy-fresh wine made mostly in the south of Italy.

SWEET REDS It's good to serve sweet red wines chilled, because it balances out the wine's sweetness.

BOBAL An up-and-coming Spanish grape that's supple and very fruity.

SPARKLING SHIRAZ You'd normally serve fizz cold, wouldn't you? So treat the bubbles in this wine the same way. The ripe Shiraz fruit will need some time to open out, so it's best to leave it for a few minutes to warm up, rather than serve it straight from the fridge.

Reds to serve 20–30 minutes or more after leaving the fridge:

GRENACHE This grape is low in tannin so it's often happy being a bit cooler. The younger the better, and for me this usually applies more to New World Grenache wines than those from Spain or France.

SYRAH/SHIRAZ Although Syrah can be high in tannin, the floral aroma and black-pepper spice is beautifully accentuated if it's served cool. Syrah from the Elqui Valley in Chile is a classic example.

MANSOIS Reds from the pocket of Marcillac in south-west France make lovely, crunchy red wines from Mansois that cry out to be a little cold because of their subtle spice.

What is 'cellar cold'?

It's just a phrase used in the wine trade to describe a wine that is noticeably cooler to the touch than room temperature, without being fridge-cold.

CABERNET SAUVIGNON

chewy •
concentrated •
meaty • plush •
smoky

SMELLS
smoky • toasty •
oaky • leathery

TASTES OF
blackcurrant •
blueberry • cherry
cinnamon •
eucalyptus • fruit
cake • jam/jelly •
liquorice • mint •
nutmeg • prune •
tobacco • vanilla

Packed with flavour, high quality and relatively easy to grow, Cabernet Sauvignon is one of the world's most important grapes. It is one of the true and original 'international' wine grapes, too, because it's grown very successfully all over the world.

Cabernet Sauvignon is French, of course, but it is not native to the region of Bordeaux as so many people think. True, Bordeaux is the region that made Cabernet Sauvignon famous, but it actually comes from further down the country, in south-west France. Plus, and this is unusual for some of the best-known grapes, both of its parent grapes are big players in the world of wine in their own right: Cabernet Franc and Sauvignon Blanc.

It might feel like the safe option, but Cabernet Sauvignon has way more going for it than just brand recognition. The dark skin of the berries gives the wine a strong colour; their thick skin adds tannin and grip in the mouth (which can help a wine to age) and it loves to be blended with other grapes. Some red grapes and styles can be flabby and soft in the mouth when they are grown and made in warm climates, but not Cab Sauv, which has a naturally high acidity that keeps its wines fresh in the mouth. It's also a huge bonus that Cabernet Sauvignon can be just as good by itself as it is when it's part of a blend.

Merlot is one of Cabernet Sauvignon's all-time-favourite blending partners and together they're a fantastic match. Bordeaux is where this blend is most famously made but it's found everywhere, from West Coast USA to Italy.

Although Cabernet Sauvignon has many high-quality credentials, that's not to say all of its wines are the pinnacle of red wine production. Cabernet Sauvignon is often made into flavoursome cheaper (more affordable) wines, too, which goes some way to explaining its popularity.

REGIONS & FLAVOURS

HOME REGION SOUTH-WEST FRANCE

There's isn't one location you can point to and say, 'Look; this is where Cabernet Sauvignon rules.' Instead, Cabernet Sauvignon makes itself useful across many of the sub-regions in south-west France, including those around the fringes of Bordeaux, like Bergerac, and further south in places like Madiran. In wines from these regions, a dollop of Cabernet Sauvignon in the blend can add colour, pedigree, potential longevity. You name it, Cabernet Sauvignon can improve it. Usually...

BORDEAUX, FRANCE

This isn't just for collectors and millionaires; Cabernet Sauvignon is one of the linchpins of red Bordeaux at all quality and price levels. And remember, all red Bordeaux is given the name 'claret', no matter what it is or how much it costs. In Bordeaux, Cabernet Sauvignon is usually blended with the region's other red grapes, such as Merlot and Cabernet Franc.

Oak and Cabernet Sauvignon are good friends, because the grape's fruit is ballsy enough to take on a fair whack of oak, but be careful with young wines as they can sometimes be quite strong in oaky tannin. Cabernet Sauvignon vineyards thrive in the part of Bordeaux known as the Left Bank (of the River Gironde). On the Right Bank, the soils are more suitable for Merlot, although both grapes exist on both banks.

When Cabernet Sauvignon dominates in a claret, it's famously powerful with blackcurrant and mint flavours.

USA

The backbone of California's serious wine reputation was built on Cabernet Sauvignon. It was made famous in the 1970s, when a blind-tasting competition of California versus Bordeaux ('The Judgement of Paris') revealed that Californian wines fared better in the results. It caused serious shockwaves through the wine community, much to the delight of the Americans and, unsurprisingly, since then, the Cabernet Sauvignon wine scene in California has gone crazy, exploded, especially in the highfalutin regions of Napa and Sonoma. These wines historically are hefty beasts that pack quite a punch, with big tannins that need time to soften out. But there have been some changes afoot in the state in general (less so in Napa) in recent years, and now the more subtle versions of Cabernet Sauvignons are also being recognized for their quality and value, such as those from Viano Vineyards. In Washington State, the USA's other main Cabernet Sauvignon hub, I usually find it less in-your-face and more fruity. The top wines are ready for drinking earlier, usually because they have less tannin. This state is definitely the place to eke out some undiscovered Cabernet Sauvignon-producing gems like Hedge's.

AUSTRALIA

Cabernet Sauvignon is one of the major red wines that helped Australia make a name for itself, and in fairness, decent, easy-drinking Cabernet Sauvignon can be found everywhere. Big in rich fruit with blackcurrant cordial-like concentration, a lot of Australian Cabernet Sauvignon (or 'Aussie Cab', as it's known) is blended with Merlot or Shiraz. Even when it's blended here, though, it retains a really distinctive character of blueberry and blackcurrant fruit, but the most obvious flavours are mint and eucalyptus.

A fashionable place to seek out top-end Cabernet Sauvignon at the moment is in Western Australia, especially the region of Margaret River, which makes very elegant wines, such as those from Cullen

Wines. Less fashionable, but still hugely respected as an area for serious Cabernet Sauvignon, is Coonawarra in South Australia. Henshke is a particular favourite producer of mine.

CHINA

Surprised to see this here? Well, because red Bordeaux has won over so many Chinese wine drinkers in recent years, they're having a crack at it themselves, and so the rate of vine planting has rocketed. If you have a chance to try these wines I'd really recommend it.

That said, China hasn't proven itself to have ideal growing conditions for Cabernet Sauvignon just yet. But the appetite for success is huge, and experienced winemakers are being drafted in from all over the world to help improve China's wine quality. It's a question of watch this space – at the moment, the region of Ningxia looks like it has the most potential.

CHILE

Cabernet Sauvignon grows especially well in Chile, so many producers here have a Cabernet Sauvignon wine in their range. Today, as Chile continues to experiment successfully with other grapes, and discover on a more specific basis what regions are suited to particular grapes, easy-going Cabernet Sauvignon is less of a focus for them, although there's no denying that Cabernet Sauvignon makes very fruity, flavoursome and usually affordable wines here. Casa Lapostolle, Viña von Siebenthal, Errázuriz, De Martino and Valdivieso wines would be on my shopping list.

THE REST OF EUROPE

France aside, Cabernet Sauvignon is a major player for some big names in Italy, especially central and southern Italy (although local grape varieties still rule here, naturally). Most famously, Cabernet Sauvignon is big in Tuscany, where it's crucial for the wines known as 'Super Tuscans'. Back in the 1960s, Super Tuscan producers decided to make wines from international grapes like Cabernet Sauvignon and Merlot, which meant they couldn't qualify for Italy's traditional quality hierarchy system. This rebellion made Cabernet Sauvignon infamous and guaranteed its place on the Italian wine scene. Plus, the wines are excellent, so they're now a firm fixture in Tuscany – and the Tuscans can charge quite a price for them, too. The most famous Super Tuscan, and for including a lot of Cabernet Sauvignon, is Sassicaia, but I'm also a huge fan of the lesser-known Castello del Terriccio Super Tuscan, called Lupicaia.

Cabernet Sauvignon is also grown throughout Spain, and is sometimes used in red Rioja, although not in large quantities. Spanish Cabernet Sauvignon is big and meaty, I usually find it to be somewhere between Bordeaux and California in style and weight in the mouth.

Below: Vineyards in Montagne de Reims, France; Opposite: St Émilion, Dordogne, France

MERLOT

creamy • juicy •
smooth • spicy •
succulent

SMELLS
gamey • leathery •
smoky

TASTES OF
beetroot/beet •
blackberry •
black cherry •
black olive • cedar •
cigar • eucalyptus •
fruit cake •
liquorice • plum •
vanilla

Merlot has plenty going for it; it's easy to pronounce, easy to drink and can be easy on the wallet, too. Merlot actually has two identities, though. It has enough character to make fleshy, fruity, easy-drinking red wines on its own (known as a single-varietal wine). It has this character because Merlot berries are relatively large, which means the juice-to-skin ratio is high, giving its wines extra-fleshy red-fruit flavour, like those you find in Chile. Or, Merlot can be an important component in blended wines, which include some of the most expensive wines in the world, like red Bordeaux, which is also known as claret, or the Super Tuscans (see pages 73–74).

The 'wing man' role that Merlot plays to Cabernet Sauvignon is seriously important because Cabernet Sauvignon can sometimes taste a bit tight on its own and needs fleshing out, making Merlot the perfect partner. Whether used as part of a blend (with any grape by the way, not just Cab Sauv), or on its own, Merlot is grown all over the world, because it's popular to drink and relatively easy to grow, making it, like Cabernet Sauvignon, another of these 'international' grapes.

REGIONS & FLAVOURS

HOME REGION BORDEAUX, FRANCE

On Bordeaux's Right Bank, where the soils are rich in clay, Merlot takes charge. It doesn't just make expensive wines from châteaux like Petrus, Angélus and Cheval Blanc; but it can and does make everyday wines, rich in black plum flavours. Merlot also plays a vital support act to Cabernet Sauvignon in making some of the most admired and expensive wines in the world. These include the First Growths in the part of Bordeaux known as the Left Bank (see page 14). Here, Merlot softens Cabernet Sauvignon to boost the fruit flavour in the wines.

CHILE

Chilean Merlot is a signature style that put Chile on the winemaking map. With tons of fruit, a soft texture and light tannins, it's uncomplicated and often very affordable. Merlot contributed to Chile's reputation as a country that could only produce cheap quaffing wines, but that's changed a lot in recent years, as Chile has branched out, growing a wide variety of grapes, including many of those featured in this book. Chilean Merlot is still big business though, and a lot of the wines are in the affordable style, packed with lots of fruit, and that still makes them a winner in many people's books. See below for its famous confusion with Carmenère.

ITALY

Although other countries are scaling back on Merlot, it's become increasingly important in Italy in recent years. You'll find most Italian

Did you know?

The grape variety Carmenère is actually what put Chilean 'Merlot' on the map. When Chilean Merlot started to become popular, much of it was actually made from Carmenère because the vines got mixed up in the vineyards.

Merlot in the north of the country. It's not massively identifiable in Italy because it is usually blended with other grapes. Plus, of course, it is most important for its role as part of the famous production of Super Tuscan wines (see page 73-74).

SPAIN

As with Italy, we think of Spain as being chock-full of its own charismatic local grape varieties, and it is, but Merlot has still pervaded its way through the red wine country of Spain with success. Like in Italy, it is used to soup up slightly wimpy red wines.

USA

Wherever Cabernet Sauvignon leads, Merlot follows. And vice versa, because one is yin to the other's yang — they make great blending partners. This means that Merlot is hugely important in California, where it is part of what is known as a Meritage blend. These wines must comprise at least two of these grapes: Cabernet Sauvignon, Merlot, Cabernet Franc, Malbec, Petit Verdot and Carmenère. They are big and rich and ripe, but with Merlot added to the mix, they're that little bit more approachable and ready for earlier drinking. But even when it's not blended with other grapes, Californian Merlot can be big, bold and rich.

In Washington State, the Merlots are generally less 'big' than those from California. They are fresher in style, but still have plenty of the grape's characteristic flavour traits, filled with black fruit, leather, aniseed and liquorice.

AUSTRALIA

Australia seems to have left Merlot well alone, although (as we know) you will find it close to wherever Cabernet Sauvignon is grown, and in the true Australian style, when Merlot is a single-varietal wine, it will be ripe, plummy and juicy.

Chateau Petrus, Pomerol, Bordeaux, France

MALBEC

creamy •
concentrated •
earthy • meaty •
perfumed • spicy

SMELLS
floral • leathery •
perfumed • smoky
spicy • toasty •
tobacco

TASTES OF
blackberry •
blackcurrant •
black olive •
black pepper •
cherry • chocolate
cinnamon •
liquorice • plum •
raspberry • truffle

The original name for Malbec – Cot, sometimes Côt – has never caught on, even though it's not exactly difficult to say. But no matter what you call it, we can't seem to get enough of this grape at the moment, thanks to its chunky handsomeness and lashings of blackcurrant fruit.

Malbec makes rich and juicy dark-red wines wherever it is produced. Although it's most famous as a varietal wine (made on its own rather than blended with other grapes), it isn't unusual to blend Malbec. Especially so in its natural home, Cahors in south-west France, where it's known as Cot or Auxerrois.

REGIONS & FLAVOURS

HOME REGION CAHORS, FRANCE
Widely believed to be the home of this grape, wines in this region must be made from at least 70% Cot, while Merlot or Tannat make up the rest of the blend. If producers don't adhere to this rule they can't put the Cahors name on the label, and they definitely don't want to miss out on that, because Cahors wines are held in high esteem, commanding some of the greatest respect of all the wines made in south-west France.

When it comes to style, Cahors wines can

be more rustic and earthy in flavour than the Malbecs you find in the southern hemisphere. They are delicious with any dish where red meat and big flavour play leading roles.

ARGENTINA

Bright, pure, full of juicy, black fruit and with creamy oak flavours – this is Argentinian Malbec in a nutshell. In fact, Malbec has been so successful in Argentina, it can now be found all over South America, from Chile to Peru. But Argentina remains the unequivocal daddy of southern hemisphere Malbec and, particularly in the region of Mendoza. To go even further, we can hone in on Mendoza's sub-region, the Uco Valley, which is fast becoming a superior Malbec Mecca. So superior, in fact, that 'Uco Valley' or 'Valle de Uco' is often proudly displayed on the bottle labels – look out for it.

Malbec has such a long history in Argentinian soil that its growers are at a distinct advantage when it comes to selecting the best fields and vines. The vineyards are at high altitudes in a hot climate, which is perfect for Malbec, and the growing season is long, meaning there are plenty of good-quality grapes.

When Malbec hit the big time in Argentina, it was mostly for single-varietal (made purely from this grape variety) Malbecs. But there's a growing trend towards making wines that are based on Malbec, with other grapes thrown in, like Cabernet Sauvignon and Merlot, all in the name of elevating the wine's complexity. Some of my favourite producers of pure Malbec include Pulenta and Achaval Ferrer.

USA

Malbec is grown all over the United States, but it's most popular in California and Washington State. In California, it's often used to beef up red blends, while in Washington it makes elegant, black-fruited wines. As in Argentina, Washington has a long growing season, but when it gets very hot, very quickly, it can lead to grapes that are high in sugar but with less depth of flavour than their Argentinian cousins.

CHILE

The first Chilean Malbec I tasted blew me away. It was made by a French winemaker and the fruit came from Casablanca Valley, the region that put Chile on the map in terms of making serious white wines. Today, the number of people making Malbec in Chile is on the up, and not just from Casablanca, either, but from vineyards all over the country. I often find Chilean Malbecs to be less full-bodied than those from Argentina, but they have an extra kick of black-pepper spice, which is very refreshing.

AUSTRALIA

As Australia endeavours to show that it's more than just a one-trick pony (that trick being Shiraz, see pages 26–31), we are now seeing more Malbec coming out of Australia. Of course Malbec and Shiraz both make big, rich, fruity wines, but from what I've tasted so far, the Australian ones, especially those from Margaret River in western Australia and Langhorne Creek in southern Australia, are worth checking out.

Did you know?

Malbec is wonderful as a rich red, but also delicious in pink wine, because it's easy to extract lots of colour and flavour from its berries and skin.

Vineyards in Mendoza, Argentina

Let's talk tannin...

Tannin is that dry, chewy coating you feel in the mouth when you take a sip of wine. It clings to teeth, the tongue and the sides of the mouth and has the same effect as tea that's had the teabag in it for too long.

Where does tannin come from?

GRAPES It's naturally present in the stems, skins and seeds of a grape. The level of tannin is usually higher in black/red grapes than white grapes.

WOOD Wines that spend time in contact with wood will pick up more tannin. When the wood is brand new, the tannin presence in wine is stronger. However, when winemakers use 'old' barrels – ones that previously contained wine – the tannins are weaker.

What does it do?

Tannin acts as a frame for a wine to develop around. It provides a chewy texture in the mouth and can improve a wine's ability to age. That's not to say that all wines that have massive tannins are going to age well for decades, just that tannin is one of the crucial components for ageing.

Want to feel less tannin?

There are two really easy ways to minimize tannin. One is to drink the wine with food. The texture of food in your mouth will lessen the chewy impact of tannin. The other is to age the wine. Tannins dissipate with time, but you have to bear in mind whether the wine has the rest of the attributes to age well – big tannins alone don't constitute a high-quality wine.

Why put wine in wood in the first place?

For two simple reasons: flavour and tannin. The flavour of wood can be critical to a wine's trademark style, as it is in red Rioja or Napa Cabernet Sauvignon. Wine can be aged in wood or fermented in wood, so for maximum flavour of the wood and tannin strength, a winemaker will do both. Oak is far and away the most popular wood used in winemaking because the flavour it imparts to the wine is favourable and because it's more watertight than other varieties of wood.

Where does the oak come from?

France and America are by far the most popular locations for sourcing oak for wine, and winemakers choose the origin of their oak based on how it will affect the wine's taste. For example, historically, red Rioja producers have always preferred American oak, but in Italy, Slavonian oak from Bosnia, Slovenia and Serbia is popular for grape varieties like Nebbiolo. American oak has a hallmark flavour of vanilla that isn't as prominent in French oak.

Do you have to use barrels?

No. A cheaper way to introduce oak influence is to suspend oak chips or oak staves (planks) in the wine, like a teabag. However, this method is widely deemed an inferior method, compared with oak barrels.

How do barrels change the flavour?

The barrels are exposed to fire and 'toasted'. Generally, there are three levels of toasting – light, medium and strong. The stronger the toast level, the more the flavour of the barrel will show through in the wine.

Did you Know?

Tannins in wine taste stronger to us when we drink wine on a flight because altitude accentuates our perception of tannin.

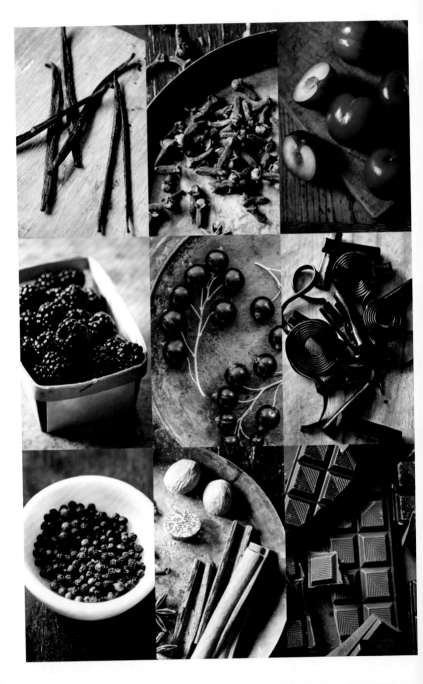

GRENACHE & FRIENDS

Red Grenache makes some of the world's most serious wines and is also one of the world's most planted wine grapes, so it trades under several names: Grenache in France, Garnacha in Spain, Garnatxa in Basque country and Canonnau in Sardinia. Yet, it still doesn't have the international respect and adoration that other grapes enjoy. In an effort to raise awareness of its significance, in 2009, a bunch of diehard fanatics created International Grenache Day on the third Friday in September, to celebrate all things Grenache.

Why have fans become noisy about Grenache? Well, partly because its plantings are sadly in decline, even though it is very important to some of the world's most significant wine hubs, like France, Spain and Italy, as well as the New World, Australia and California especially. It's bizarre that the plantings of Grenache are down, because the grape can produce fantastic red wines in environments that are hot and arid, so it functions – even better, it makes delicious wines – in a climate where other grapes would give up (and they may well give up in future as the Earth gets warmer). Grenache also has relatively low acidity, which is especially useful when it comes to pairing with food.

Sounds too good to be true? Well, Grenache is not without imperfections. You have to watch out for its alcohol level for a start, because it's a grape that ripens late, allowing the sugar levels (that convert to alcohol) to creep up. The grape's hang time on the vine can also increase the level of tannin, meaning Grenache-based wines need a little longer in the bottle before they are drunk to mellow those tannins.

As the title of this section suggests, Grenache is happiest when blended with other grapes, especially with Syrah/Shiraz and Mourvèdre, which is why you sometimes see GSM (Grenache, Syrah/Shiraz, Mourvèdre) on labels. Three of its best friends are Mourvèdre, Carignan and Cinsaut.

MOURVÈDRE/MONASTRELL/MATARO

This grape loves to be warm in the summer and not too cold in the winter, which is why it's never grown too far from the Mediterranean, although Australians like it in GSM too. It can be made as a varietal wine, one that's rich in fruit and bold in flavour. It adds three things to these wines: tannin thanks to its thick skin; a sweet and intense blackcurrant flavour; and finally, alcohol.

CARIGNAN/CARIGNANO/CARIÑENA/MAZUELO

Carignan isn't really in favour at the moment, and is often passed over for other grape varieties, even though it can be useful to add acidity and colour to red wine. It can also make some deliciously fragrant varietal wines, especially in the South of France where, at its best, Carignan grows on bush vines which are old, and this age adds complexity to the grape's flavour – so much so that 'bush vine' is now a familiar phrase on wine labels. Morocco and Israel are both Carignan-growing regions worth watching out for.

CINSAULT/CINSAUT *Say it: san-so*

Cinsault is starting to become a bit of a modern star after a tumultuous history of popularity. But now it's hugely back in favour in South Africa, where it's often blended with other southern French grapes, such as Cabernet Sauvignon, to make a really juicy, easy-drinking red.

REGIONS, GRAPES & FLAVOURS

FRANCE

RHÔNE VALLEY This valley runs from Lyon to Avignon and is split in two on the winemaking map. While Syrah/Shiraz is the only red grape permitted in the northern Rhône (most people drop the 'Valley'), the southern Rhône red wines are all about blends.

CHÂTEAUNEUF-DU-PAPE, GIGONDAS, VACQUEYRAS & CÔTES DU RHÔNE
Grenache, Syrah/Shiraz, Mourvèdre, Cinsaut

Grenache rules in the southern Rhône, and especially in its most famous region, Châteauneuf-du-Pape, which produces bold, rich, earthy reds that need to be aged for a good few years, roughly eight, to be enjoyed at their best. Amazingly, Châteauneuf (the 'du-Pape' is often dropped) makes about as much wine as the whole of the northern Rhône put together, and is a wine region especially famous for its soil. It is covered with smooth boulders called *galets rouges*, that store heat well for the vines in the ground and so produces riper grapes. Châteauneuf wines can be made from 18 different grapes, and each producer has its own magic recipe for the 'right' Châteauneuf that's rich in flavour, dark in colour and high in meaty tannins.

Gigondas, just north-east of Châteauneuf, makes wines that are comprised of up to 80% Grenache. Like Châteauneuf, these are wines that shouldn't be drunk early, and are usually at their peak when five to 10 years old. They're dark, rich, smooth, full of black fruits and peppery spice. You will find some nice, dry, punchy rosés made in Gigondas, too.

Vacqueyras is the newbie region. Nestled between Châteauneuf and Gigondas, it produces white, rosé and red wines but really majors in red Grenache blends. They're big, herbal-flavoured wines, with lots of black plum fruit and often black pepper notes because Syrah/Shiraz is Grenache's main partner here.

Côtes du Rhône is a regional category for wines that span the Rhône Valley. It is one of those prolific names on restaurant wine lists because it's very versatile with food. Côtes du Rhône-Villages is its

---

Did you know?

You can also get white Châteauneuf-du-Pape. It's not as common as the red, but it's growing in popularity and can be made from any of the following grapes: Grenache Blanc, Clairette, Roussanne, Bourboulenc and Picardan.

superior, and these have a minimum of 40% Grenache in them. They're full of juicy plum and blackcurrant fruit, and are designed for drinking relatively early. They are sumptuous and very drinkable red wines.

LANGUEDOC-ROUSSILLON
Grenache, Syrah/Shiraz, Mourvèdre, Carignan
These juicy red wines have improved enormously in the last 20 years. Syrah/Shiraz wears the crown in terms of importance, but Grenache is also a big deal. Producers in this region are experimental with their wines and a Languedoc-Roussillon blend is often my go-to choice of red in a restaurant. The best Grenache blends not only have deep, black fruit with gentle tannins, but they capture the woody herbs of the area, too, especially thyme. Regions worth looking out for are Côtes Catalanes, Corbiéres, Faugères, Fitou, Minervois and Saint-Chinian.

TAVEL Grenache is hugely important in Tavel, mostly for its spicy and serious dry rosé (see pages 144-151).

SPAIN
RIOJA & NAVARRA
Garnacha, Tempranillo
Garnacha is incredibly important in Spain's most famous wine region, Rioja. It plays a lead (but not the leading) role alongside Tempranillo (see pages 64-69) as the framework of most red Rioja. Loved for their rich, red-fruit flavours, white-pepper spice, and herbal and spicy notes; they often taste of vanilla and chocolate. Garnacha is especially important in Rioja Baja, the easternmost of the three Rioja sub-regions, furthest from the sea, where it is hotter. Next door to Rioja, Navarra does a good job at making red wines that are similar to red Rioja in style but at a slightly lower price. Navarra, however, is really known for its Grenache-filled *rosado* (rosé) wines (see pages 144-151).

PRIORAT
Cariñena, Garnacha, Syrah/Shiraz
A relatively recent success, this Catalonian region south-west of Barcelona, is a great story of a wine region being revived. It's a super-swanky winemaking area that is the only Spanish region other than Rioja to be awarded the highest wine classification (DOCa). Here, Garnacha is best when blended with Cariñena, and a lot of praise is awarded to the unique slate soil, called llicorella (*say it: yickor-ey-a*). Red wines from Priorat are dense with ripe black fruit but also have a liquorice spice and often a fair dose of chocolate flavour, too. They command a pretty big price and are not meant to be drunk early. Give them at least eight years to mellow.

ITALY
Cannonau, Carignano
Sardinia is the only stronghold of Cannonau (Grenache) in Italy, and some people even think it's the birthplace of the variety. This is one of the places where you can find 100% Cannonau, made into dry or sweet wines, or blended with Carignano. The dry wines are big, beefy, even jammy in flavour, and given the heat on the island, it's hardly surprising that these wines often reach alcohol levels of 15% ABV (alcohol by volume). If you're having a barbecue, a big and rustic Cannonau di Sardegna is just the wine you need.

USA
In both California and Washington, rich, spicy and generous Grenache-blended cult wines are popping up. These are far more interesting than any of the very cheap Grenache found in California. The better-quality blends in both states are rich in black cherry and have a lovely liquorice spice. Think Châteauneuf, but bigger!

AUSTRALIA
Grenache, Shiraz, Mataro
Grenache is hot property in Australia right now. And so it should be, because Grenache's love of hot and arid conditions makes Australia a

no-brainer of a place to make it. Again, it is shown at its best when blended with other grapes, especially Shiraz and Mataro – the Australians are big fans of that acronym GSM. South Australia is where Grenache and its blending friends rule, and I'd earmark McLaren Vale, Barossa Valley and Langhorne Creek as regions with intense GSM wines.

ISRAEL
Grenache, Syrah/Shiraz, Mourvèdre, Carignan
There's a slow but exciting change happening here. Many quality-conscious Israeli producers now see the potential in Grenache and friends which are often more suited to Israeli conditions than Bordeaux grapes. They're rich and meaty wines with a smoky spice.

Châteauneuf du Pape vineyard, France

SPANISH REDS

People who choose nothing but Rioja for their Spanish red wine fix are missing a trick. Not that there's anything wrong with Rioja, of course, but it's a shame to pigeonhole a country as having one decent red wine when it has so much more to offer. Spain, like other Old World countries, has upped its game in recent years. It still makes masses of wine, and some of it can be pretty mediocre, but just as with Italy, these days there's more of a focus on quality rather than quantity — a welcome move in any wine-lover's book.

The modern improvement in quality of Spanish red wines has involved a few things: tweaking grape blends (but not beyond the point of recognition), championing forgotten grape varieties and regions that have great potential, as well as adopting new techniques to make red wines more thoughtfully, rather than just, say, throwing loads of oak at them.

There's also a more thoughtful approach to vine planting. For Spain, this is really about altitude, because across much of Spain, the ground temperature is just too hot to grow good grapes for wine. So today, vines are increasingly found at higher altitudes where it's cooler, and this usually means the wines both taste fresher and will be lower in alcohol.

TEMPRANILLO *Say it: temp-ra-knee-oh*

Tempranillo is the backbone red wine grape in Spain, and although it's also important as Tinta Roriz in Portugal, it is now one of the popular red grapes being produced in New World winemaking hot spots.

Tempranillo loves hot and arid conditions. It soaks up the heat without necessarily accumulating too much sugar, which means it doesn't always reach the same alcohol heights as Garnacha (see pages 56-63). In general, Tempranillo's flavour is more about leather and spice than the bucket loads of fruit like in Garnacha and other red grapes. The earthy flavours can be gorgeously plush, and because

Tempranillo doesn't have loads of natural acidity, it often makes wines that are mellow rather than fresh. If producers want to perk up the acidity in Tempranillo, they'll simply blend it with another grape – it's very cooperative and is happy being blended.

It used to be possible to pick Spanish Tempranillo out in a crowd thanks to the American oak barrels, which gave the wines a trademark vanilla flavour. Today, it's not so easy to spot for several reasons: there's increasingly more Tempranillo grown around the world; wines from Spanish regions other than Rioja are now more available to us; and the use of oak in Tempranillo has changed – French oak is now more popular, plus it spends significantly less time ageing in oak than it used to.

RIOJA

It might be in northern central Spain, or – if you're a foodie – due south of San Sebastián, but Rioja is the epicentre of Spanish red wine for many people, and Tempranillo plays the leading role. As a region, Rioja really hit the big time in terms of being an acceptable and revered wine in the 1970s. Since then, it's been on a bit of a rollercoaster ride with its style. In the '80s and '90s, there was a bigger emphasis on quality rather than quantity, more French barrels were used and Tempranillo spent less time in oak. These two changes in winemaking techniques are what those in the industry refer to as 'modern Rioja', but that doesn't necessarily mean they're better wines. Today, the region is changing again, as producers try to re-authenticate red Rioja by highlighting its unique identity. This in part means returning to some of the older methods, albeit with a modern twist. Whether it's modern or not, Tempranillo shines through in red Rioja as a smooth and supple wine with flavours of leather and tobacco.

Tempranillo is grown in all three of Rioja's sub-regions: Alta, Alavesa and Baja, although Baja is the easternmost and hottest sub-region so Garnacha is more common there (see pages 56-63). Tempranillo makes up about two-thirds of Rioja's vineyards, but it's often blended with other grapes, the most common being Garnacha, but Mazuelo and Monastrell are also important.

NAVARRA

Just like its neighbour Rioja, Tempranillo is important in blended red wines here, although it's nowhere near as important to the region as Garnacha. Still, they make wines that aren't too dissimilar to red Rioja, with that leather, spice and tobacco flavour, but they're generally slightly lighter in style.

CATALONIA

Tempranillo is one of the most important varieties across all of Catalonia's sub-regions, although many parts of this area are embracing 'international' grapes like Cabernet Sauvignon, too.

VALDEPEÑAS

The baking heat of southern central Spain has seen a revival of red wines recently, and Tempranillo, known locally as Cencibel, is making some smooth and smoky reds without being heavy or serious. It's still early days here, but an area to keep an eye on.

RIBERA DEL DUERO

This is where Spanish wine got modern. Ribera del Duero (often shortened to 'Ribera') is the region that climbed the social wine echelons quickly in the 1990s. And that's all thanks to Tempranillo, which doesn't just have one name here, but two: Tinto Fino and Tinto del País.

Excitingly different to red Rioja, the Tempranillo in Ribera makes wines that are fruitier than Rioja, not in a sappy-fruit way, but in a deep, intense and concentrated way — a way that makes you sit up and

Not all Tempranillo is made in Spain...

Tempranillo thrives in places that can withstand hot conditions. This means places like Portugal, America and Australia can make fantastic Tempranillo. In Portugal, it is called 'Tinta Roriz' or 'Aragonez' (or 'Aragonês'), depending on where it's made.

take notice. This is not only because of the extra fruit, but because they usually taste more lively and pretty fresh, too, for Tempranillo. Ribera is further inland than Rioja and more continental, with cooler nights allowing the grape's flavour to develop slowly. These wines are capable of extended ageing – the best ones aren't ready until they're at least 10 years old.

Producers to look out for are Torres with their Ribera wine Celeste, Abadía Retuerta, Pesquera and finally Vega Sicilia, which is Spain's most iconic winery and makes a cult wine. Vega Sicilia's wines are made from Tempranillo and are typically blended with grapes that are famous in Bordeaux, like Cabernet Sauvignon and Merlot. Unico is the top Vega Sicilia wine and reaches a hefty price. It's mostly Tempranillo, and isn't usually released until 10 years after it's made.

BOBAL

Spain's secondmost planted red grape hasn't made any headlines internationally yet, but that could soon change because the wine community is getting a bit frisky about it. It has a bit of a bad-kid-come-good history because in the past, Bobal was a popular grape for bulk wine production, but now there's more thoughtful planting of the vines at higher altitudes, which gives extra freshness to the wines. The best of this new breed of Bobals make reds that taste of plums, but the masterstroke is their smooth and supple character combined with decent acidity, all of which make them very good drinking wines rather than wines for keeping. It is this chirpy, fruity character that sees Bobal increasingly made into pink wine, too.

Regional namesakes

Remember, in Spain, like the rest of Europe, the region where wine is made often gives the name to the wine style too, rather than the grape varieties from which the wine is made. For example, Rioja, Ribera del Duero, Toro, Navarra...

Mostly, Bobal is found in the regions that head out from the heart of central Spain towards Valencia, such as Manchuela, Utiel Requena and the winemaking area named Valencia (not to be confused with the city). Try the Bobal from Bodegas y Viñedos Ponce, if you can.

MENCÍA *Say it: menth-eeya*

This grape makes red wines with attitude and doesn't need to be slathered in oak or blended with other varieties to prove itself. Grown in north-west Spain, Mencía can make ripe and fruity reds as well as firm and serious ones, but whichever style it is, they're both seriously delicious.

Some of the regions where this grape is best known include Ribeira Sacra, Monterrei and Valdeorras, where you can also find the lovely white grape, Godello. The most exciting Mencía hotspot, though, is the region of Bierzo. This is where the floral bouquet of Mencía and pretty, perky juicy beetroot/beet flavour is captured at its best. Palacios, which is a producer name more familiar in Priorat (see page 62), invested in the Bierzo region and now makes some truly great wines. While Pena das Donas and Raúl Pérez are lesser-known names, they also make fantastic Mencía.

GRACIANO

This is increasing in popularity and peps up a wine with its floral aroma and fresh acidity. It also has good tannins, so it's a useful grape to help a Rioja age well.

INTERNATIONAL GRAPES

It's not completely unheard of to find international grapes in Spanish reds, including some Cabernet Sauvignon skulking around in Rioja's vineyards.

ITALIAN REDS

If you're looking for wines that reek of authenticity and flavour, look no further than Italy. While I'm objective in my work, in my downtime there's no question that I have a huge personal interest in Italian wine. In fact, it's not uncommon in my house on Christmas day for all of the wines we drink to come from Italy; from fizz at the start of the day through to sticky wine at the end. This chapter pays homage to Italian reds, and there's no shortage of wines to pay homage to. One of the beautiful things about Italian wines is all those inimitable local grape varieties, which make this country a hive of delicious, distinctive red wines.

NEBBIOLO
BAROLO & BARBARESCO, PIEDMONT

One of the jewels in Italy's crown, Nebbiolo, makes mesmerizing red wines. Its trademark character is the powerful aroma, which is like crushing black peppercorns in a pestle and mortar, then squishing in a few sour black cherries. Its home is in the north-east, Piedmont. Here it makes hedonistic red wines in the villages of Barolo and Barbaresco (which are also names of wine styles). Barolo is thought to be more meaty, whereas Barbaresco is generally prettier. Both styles are high in tannin so, in my experience, they should never be drunk very young, and can take as long as a decade to soften enough to enjoy. But they're so gorgeous we're probably all a bit guilty of drinking them too young.

BARBERA
PIEDMONT

Another red grape that's local and special to Piedmont, even though you can find it in other pockets of Italy. Small pockets. Barbera usually gives its name to the regions where it's grown, the most popular being Barbera d'Asti and Barbera d'Alba. Of these two, Barbera is more of a speciality in the region of Asti, but it's Barbera d'Alba that usually costs more. A bit like Nebbiolo, Barbera can cross the boundaries from being an easy-drinking red with dense, cherry flavours and softer raspberry flavours, to a richer wine. Conterno and Fantino make some truly gorgeous Barberas.

SANGIOVESE *Say it: sanjo-vair-zee*
CHIANTI, TUSCANY &... EVERYWHERE

Sangiovese, or derivations of it (this grape mutates at the drop of a hat) can be found all over Italy. But it's most famous and most revered in Tuscany, especially in Chianti, which is a sub-region within Tuscany, as well as the name of its wine style, of course.

Chianti is split further into sub-regions, and of these, Chianti Classico is widely recognized as the highest-quality, and will therefore usually cost more than a wine that's labelled just as 'Chianti'. These wines can be very good value for money, but it can also be a bit of a gamble because people feel safe choosing the brand Chianti, so some wines can get away with being not quite as good as they should be. Chiantis, when good, are full of cherry fruit and often have a delicious aroma of tomatoes and oregano. They can be quite versatile with food, too, so are popular on restaurant wine lists, especially because the Chianti brand recognition is very strong around the world.

BRUNELLO
MONTALCINO, TUSCANY

Remember I talked about Sangiovese mutating? Brunello is the perfect case in point. Montalcino is also in Tuscany and its Brunello di Montalcino wines are a bit like Sangiovese Chiantis on steroids. They're bigger and meatier with strong tannins when the wines are young, so you need to give them a few years to smooth out. Want a cheaper, younger-drinking but still tasty red from this region? Try a Rosso di Montalcino.

MONTEPULCIANO
ABRUZZO

Montepulciano d'Abruzzo is a juicy red wine without too much tannin and lots of cherry fruit. It's a no-brainer red for wine lists, although it's hardly ever a wine to keep for ageing.

PRIMITIVO
PUGLIA

Primitivo is a grape that has a super-dark colour and becomes a wine that's full of liquorice spice and very thick, concentrated cherry flavours. It's unashamedly full-on and packed with flavour. But be careful; it can be quite high in alcohol. I once heard a winemaker say, 'If Primitivo is less than 15% ABV (alcohol by volume) it isn't evenly balanced' – I wouldn't necessarily agree, but be warned!

NERO D'AVOLA & NERELLO MASCALESE
SICILY

Nero d'Avola is a grape that's largely used in the making of everyday-drinking wines. It's good on its own, and brings lots of big, fresh, black-fruit flavour to the party, with an extra-dry kick of cumin and paprika.

Nerello Mascalese's arrival on the world stage is a fairly recent one, but it hasn't taken long to show everyone the quality of the wines it can make, elevating Sicily's position from its high-volume, low-quality image of the past. The grape name isn't always displayed, but if a wine says 'Etna Rosso', you can be pretty sure it will have a large dollop of Nerello Mascalese in the mix. It is also often blended with its lesser-quality sibling, Nerello Cappuccio. Etna Rossos have lovely, soft raspberry flavours and are like a cross between Nebbiolo and Pinot Noir.

SUPER TUSCANS

A quick bit of history here, because Super Tuscans are the exception to the Italian wine rule. Back in the 1960s, a bunch of producers boldly started making top-end wine from grapes that were not local to the region – international grapes like Cabernet Sauvignon and Merlot. This meant that no matter how good the wines were, they weren't eligible to attain the DOCG status – the highest quality category in Italy. This didn't matter to these pioneering producers though, and rather than people thinking they were lesser-quality, their fame and adoration only grew because of their notoriety. Famous Super Tuscan names include

Sassicaia, Ornellaia and Tignanello, and these wines are rich and dense, and do a brilliant job of being both identifiable as Cabernet Sauvignon and Merlot, but also of honing the slickness of Italy. These wines are iconic and made in small volume – in other words, they're never cheap.

CORVINA, MOLINARA & RONDINELLA
VENETO

Veneto's most famous wine, Valpolicella, is a refreshing red wine that's frisky, full of cherries and has an unusual twist of marzipan to it. It's made from a blend of local grapes, Corvina, Molinara and Rondinella. Corvina is usually thought of as being the best quality, as well as the most important of these grapes, so it is always the most prominent. Amarone di Valpolicella, usually shortened to just 'Amarone', is made in a slightly different way – the grapes are left to shrivel up and dehydrate, so the sugars concentrate inside the grape. This often means the wine tastes more concentrated than other Valpolicellas, replacing the cherry flavours with raisins. The increase in sugar also means this wine has higher alcohol levels. In fact, the law stipulates that Amarone must be a minimum of 14% ABV.

Italian regions giving names to red wine styles

In Italy, as in other European countries, it is often the region where a wine is produced that lends its name to a wine style as opposed to the name of the prominent grape. Some use both, like the Barberas, Barbera d'Asti and Barbera d'Alba. This is less true of Italian white wine styles, where the names principally highlight the grapes and occasionally add on the region. Here are a few names to watch out for, alongside the grapes used to make them, to help you recognize what's what in Italian red wines.

Region & Style	Grape
Barolo	Nebbiolo
Barbaresco	Nebbiolo
Chianti	Sangiovese
Etna (Rosso)	Nerello Mascalese, Nerello Cappuccio
Valpolicella	Corvina, Molinara, Rondinella

Vineyard in Montalcino, Tuscany

FLAGSHIP REDS

As well as all of the other red wine styles featured in this book, there are some benchmark grapes that certain regions champion to make their flagship styles. Here, I take a look at some of the most important grapes and wines.

ZINFANDEL
CALIFORNIA

Discussing Zinfandel's origin and parentage is a bit like watching 'The Jerry Springer Show'. There have been claims, counter-claims, confusion and disagreements. Now, it's conclusive. Zinfandel is the same grape as Primitivo in Puglia, but it actually hails from the Croatian Dalmatian Coast.

But Zinfandel is famous for more than just disputes. In California, it's taken rosé to a new level. White Zinfandel or Zinfandel Blush is an incredible pink wine success although it's also largely responsible for the widely-held belief that all rosés are sweet.

As a dry red wine, Zinfandel is taken much more seriously. And it's a whopper, too. In fact, Ravenswood, a much-respected producer of Zinfandel in California, uses the tag line 'No Wimpy Wines', which gives you an idea of its power and strength. Usually a combination of spicy red fruit with leather and liquorice, good red 'Zin' producers include Ravenswood, Seghesio and Turley.

PINOTAGE
SOUTH AFRICA

A divisive grape that's often referred to as South Africa's flagship red. It was created in Stellenbosch in the early 20th century and is a cross of Pinot Noir with Cinsaut (South Africans used to call Cinsaut 'Hermitage', hence the hybrid name). Pinotage makes macho wines that are meaty, rich, smoky and really quite tannic. They are barbecue wines that work with grilled red meat. It's divisive because it had a tendency to taste of things like burnt rubber. However, the general quality of Pinotage has improved in recent years, and in fact, when I was last in South Africa, I tasted several really good styles – the best I'd ever tasted. If you can get hold of them, try the Pinotages from Rijk's, Bellingham and Groot Constantia.

Most recently, and controversially, red Pinotage has been seasoned with a very deliberate coffee or chocolate flavour (achieved through oak), giving producers the opportunity to give names to their wines like Barista and Cuppapinoccinotage.

CARMENÈRE *Say it: carmenair*
CHILE

Never has a case of mistaken wine identity been more famous than that of Carmenère in Chile, where for years it was accidentally confused with and identified as Merlot. What's bizarre is that, even though the Chilean wine boom happened on the back of 'Merlot', today people continue to drink it, except now it actually is Merlot, and not Carmenère.

Carmenère actually comes from Bordeaux, although it's hardly used there these days. In its newest adopted land it makes some fantastically rich and flavoursome red wines. Depending on the heat of the area in which it's grown, its flavours can range from having a herbal-green flavour of black fruit to spicy chocolate at its richest. Names to look out for include De Martino and Marques de Casa Concha.

GAMAY
BEAUJOLAIS, FRANCE

Make way for Gamay in your wine rack or fridge – this grape makes one of the most versatile wines around: Beaujolais. Beaujolais can be so juicy it's practically bursting out of your mouth, or it can be earthy and savoury.

Like many other French regions there is a quality hierarchy in Beaujolais. In its most basic form, Beaujolais (the wine style) can be a sappy, red-fruited wine that needs to be drunk within one year. Beaujolais-Villages is a step up in quality and can be kept for longer, say three to four years – these are often really good value for money.

Cru Beaujolais lists the names of the crus (the 10 villages in the region that produce the highest-quality Gamay) on the label, including Brouilly and Fleurie, Juliénas, Morgon and Moulin-à-Vent. These wines can get pretty serious, and can even age by as much as 10 years, although I think they're often at their best when they're five to eight years old. 'Beaujolais Nouveau' is a special term given to a Beaujolais that's released in the November of each year, very soon after the wine has been made. These are unoaked, so are very light and fruity wines.

The freshness, upfront fruit and lack of heavy tannin in Beaujolais make it a very food-friendly wine. Good producers include Henry Fessy, Jean-Paul Thévenet, Château Grange Cochard and Domaine de Prion.

SWITZERLAND

Gamay is very popular in the French-speaking part of Switzerland and Pinot Noir rules in German-speaking Switzerland. Sometimes these two grapes are even blended, especially in wines from Dôle. Wherever it's made, the cool conditions of Switzerland mean that its Gamay gives a pure, fragrant and raspberry-flavoured wine which makes for supple, easy drinking.

Why is Beaujolais so juicy?

The Gamay in Beaujolais doesn't just achieve serious levels of fruitiness because of the grape; it's boosted by a method of fermentation that produces wines that are meant to be drunk early. This is called 'carbonic maceration'. It involves the fermentation of the grape juice inside each individual grape, which is different to the traditional method of fermentation, where grapes are crushed to release the juice and then all the juice ferments in a big tank.

TANNAT
URUGUAY

Uruguay is not technically the 'home' of this grape, but it has adopted it as its signature style. As the name suggests, tannat makes pretty tannic wines, plus they often have good acidity. Tannat's home is actually Madiran in south-west France, and that region makes some delicious, mineral, fresh but ballsy red wine. But, if you compare the tannins of wines made from Tannat in Madiran to those in Uruguay, you'll generally see a softer side to the South American wines, thanks to the warmer climate. The best Uruguayan Tannats really need plenty of fruit to show through beyond the grip of tannin and freshness of acidity in the mouth. De Lucca and Juanicó are two great producers.

BLAUFRÄNKISCH *Say it: blauw-fran-kish*
AUSTRIA

There's a real buzz in the air surrounding Austria's flagship red grape. Although I call it the flagship red grape, another red grape called Zweigelt is actually the most planted in Austria. The style of Blaufränkisch has changed for the better since the mid-1980s, when producers threw loads of oak at the grape, stopping its flavours from shining through. Today, the use of oak on Blaufränkisch is much more sensitive, meaning it can finally show its 'sense of place'; its character. A very refreshing red wine without being aggressive in acidity, it stays fresh even in warmer years. I think Blaufränkisch is delicious when it's just a few years old, but many producers think it tastes at its best several years after it's made. It isn't a cheap wine to make, so you won't find any budget bottles on the shelves, but it's worth the money, especially those from Wachter-Wiesler, Triebaumer, Umathum and Heinrich Gernot & Keike.

TOURIGA NACIONAL *Say it: tooreegah nass-ion-ahl*
PORTUGAL

One of the most important red grapes for Port, Touriga Nacional has been thrust into the limelight in recent years as the backbone of some of Portugal's finest red wines. Touriga Nacional usually needs to be fleshed out with another Portuguese native red grape, like Tinta Cão or Touriga Franca, but it's still the main reason why these dark and rich red wines have such an attractive pure, blackcurrant, floral aroma. They're bold and rich reds with very distinctive characters, especially from producers Wine & Soul, Quinta do Noval and Quinta do Vale Maria.

PLAVAC MALI *Say it: plavatz mahlee*
CROATIA

Plavac Mali loves the heat, although it's made in southern and central Dalmatia, as well as on the islands. The best wines are made from grapes grown on the southern Kras slopes, where they're in full view of the sun. These can make big and tannic wines, and they're not shy on alcohol, either; sometimes they can reach as much as (gulp) 16% ABV. As a big red wine, though, they can be delicious and intense, and there's an attractive distinctive quality to this grape. It smells of dried herbs and flowers, while in the mouth it's very rich and often tastes of figs and prunes as well as chocolate and vanilla.

AGIORGITIKO *Say it: ah-your-yee-te-koh*
GREECE

Greece's most widely planted red makes every kind of wine, from funky, fruity rosé to deep-flavoured and serious reds that are worth ageing. It's best as a red wine that's rich and spicy, and tastes of currants and liquorice. It's most famously made in the Peloponnese district of Nemea, where the producer Gaia is one of the finest.

WHITE

The magic of white wine begins with its aromas for me;
that wonderful sensory kaleidoscope that takes your
memory on all sorts of journeys. And while the
'aromatic' grapes do all this without even trying, less
aromatic grapes, such as Chardonnay and Chenin Blanc,
make their mark on the palate instead, drawing you in
with flavours and textures that can be just as alluring
and comforting as those of red wines.

CHARDONNAY

CHARACTERISTICS
chewy • concentrated • creamy • elegant • fresh • smoky • waxy

SMELLS
appley • floral • grassy • herbaceous • nutty • oaky • smoky • toasty • waxy

TASTES OF
bacon • biscuit/cookie • brioche • butter • caramel • honey • lemon • melon • nuts • pastry • peach • pineapple • vanilla

I'm convinced there's a Chardonnay for everyone, even if it is one of those grapes that people seem to love or hate. Chardonnay's home is Burgundy, but because it's grown all over the world, and because it can be such a blank canvas, it's also pretty happy when blended with other grapes. Like it or loathe it, Chardonnay is one of the highest-quality wine grapes around.

It's one of the most popular grapes in the world, but because Chardonnay is naturally pretty neutral, it gets most of its flavour during the winemaking process, and there are two common ways to boost its flavour.

When you expose Chardonnay to oak, in barrels or by soaking the wine on wooden staves (planks), it soaks up the flavour like a sponge. This means that the winemaker has to be careful about the type of wood used when producing Chardonnay (see page 54). Chardonnay can go through the alcoholic fermentation in oak or it can be aged after fermentation. Winemakers who want lots of oaky flavour in their Chardonnay will do both.

For maximum richness in flavour – in addition to the oak – winemakers will let Chardonnay rest on its lees. Lees are the yeast deposits that are created after the wine goes through fermentation, so they add a yeasty flavour of bread and biscuits/cookies to the wine. Lees are also really important in contributing to the texture of Chardonnay in the mouth. More lees means more chewiness.

REGIONS & FLAVOURS

HOME REGION BURGUNDY, FRANCE

I'll happily confess it took me some time to get to grips with white Burgundy. All that buttery, toasty, nutty richness used to feel old-fashioned and heavy, but now I'm a total convert, so even if it doesn't work for you the first time around, I really recommend to keep trying rather than shutting the door on it. Burgundian Chardonnay can have serious complexity and has a good ability to age. Chardonnay is *the* white wine grape of Burgundy and especially in the southern half of the main strip, the region called Côte de Beaune.

CHABLIS, FRANCE

There's much debate about whether this is part of Burgundy or not. Technically, it is in the same region, but if someone is referring to white Burgundy, that usually doesn't include Chablis. The reason it's so different in style is geographic as much as anything else. Chablis is much further north and cooler than the main stretch of Burgundy, so the wines usually have a fresher bite to them.

The term 'Chablis' refers to the general wine region, the town of Chablis itself, one of the hierarchies in the wine classification system *and* the name of the general wine style, so it's no wonder people get confused about Chablis. In descending order, the hierarchy categories

labelling white Burgundy

In descending order of prestige, white Burgundy (Chardonnay) is labelled: Grand Cru; Premier Cru; (The name of a village), for example Meursault; Bourgogne.

run as follows: 'Grand Cru' then 'Premier Cru', followed by 'Chablis', then 'Petit Chablis'. Very generally speaking, the Chardonnays of these two highest classifications will usually have oak influence, while the lower two usually won't. And as for producers, some of my favourites include Moreau-Naudet and Vincent Dampt.

CHAMPAGNE, FRANCE

I can't emphasize enough the importance of Chardonnay in Champagne. It's one of the region's three main grapes and is the only white one of those three. It gives Champagne a floral fragrance, and extra crispness in the mouth as well as the ability to age for a long time. When Champagne is made purely from Chardonnay it's called a 'Blanc de Blancs', roughly translated as 'white wine made from white grapes'. Some of my favourite Blanc de Blancs Champagnes come from the houses of Charles Heidsieck, Delamotte and Larmandier-Bernier.

SPAIN

Chardonnay has become an important addition to the production of Cava, Spain's most famous sparkling wine. Whether it's blended with Pinot Noir, with native Spanish grapes, or used on its own, Chardonnay has really contributed to the improved quality of a lot of Cavas.

ENGLAND

Chardonnay is hugely important in English fizz in much the same way as it is important in Champagne. As this style of wine increases its international renown, so, too, does the amount of Chardonnay being planted, especially on England's south coast. We're now spoilt for choice. Coates & Seely in Hampshire, Wiston Estate, also in Hampshire, and Nyetimber in West Sussex all make delicious Blanc de Blancs.

FRANCIACORTA, ITALY

Give Franciacorta a go. If you like Champagne and Italian wine, I feel sure you won't be disappointed, because Franciacorta is Italy's delicious answer to Champagne. And like Champagne, Franciacorta is the name of the region in Lombardy as well as the wine style made there. Chardonnay is the most popular grape used in Franciacorta. My tip is to look out for Satèn, a style of Franciacorta that has very silky-soft bubbles. It's fresh but also very food-friendly, and still (amazingly!) unknown outside of Italy. I really like the Franciacortas made by Fratelli Berlucchi, Monte Rossa and Bellavista. Still wines made from Chardonnay in the Franciacorta region have a different name, Curtefranca, and these can be very tasty, too.

AUSTRALIA

Australia's done a great job at toning down its Chardonnay in recent years, and although oak is still used, usually it's nowhere near as sickly or in-your-face as it used to be. Elegant Chardonnays can be found all over the country now, but one of my favourite regions is the Mornington Peninsula in Victoria, where Chardonnays can be super-refined. Here, I always enjoy Yabby Lake wines. But let's not forget western Australia either, where L.A.S. Vino and Cloudburst are names to look out for. In Tasmania, it's cool enough to make fresh and zingy sparkling wine from Chardonnay. Jansz makes lovely sparkling wine there.

NEW ZEALAND

Chardonnay has been a buzzword in New Zealand for some time now. The climate's freshness makes deliciously clear and crisp Chardonnay, often with good melon and apple fruit flavours. One of the best things about Chardonnay made here is the consistency. Some regions have more experience than others in making this grape, but all the regions seem to be excited about the potential of Chardonnay, and I'm just as enthusiastic as they are. Of the NZ Chardonnays I've tasted, I've really enjoyed those from Kumeu River and Felton Road.

USA

If you like your Chardonnay smoky, toasty and rich with bacon-fat flavours, Napa is a great place to start, although the coolness of Sonoma makes some truly delicious and sophisticated Chardonnays as well. Outside of California, Washington State has some charming Chardonnays with a buttery richness and salty tang.

SAUVIGNON BLANC

CHARACTERISTICS
fresh • herbal • juicy • sour • tangy vibrant • zesty

SMELLS
floral • grassy • herbaceous • perfumed • zesty

TASTES OF
asparagus • elderflower • grapefruit • lemon lime • mango • nettle • passion fruit • pea • peach • pear

France is the home of Sauvignon Blanc, but New Zealand is where its style trends begin. When New Zealand sprang onto the wine scene back in the 1980s, its Sauvignon Blanc was hard to ignore, thanks to its insanely tropical fruit flavours.

Today, New Zealand Sauvignon Blanc has become so universally loved that even the more traditional Sauvignon Blanc regions are making wines in a copycat style.

Sauvignon Blanc isn't fussy about where it grows and it's always packed with flavour, making it a hugely popular wine grape wherever it's made. Plus it can be made into anything: dry or sweet, still or sparkling.

REGIONS & FLAVOURS

HOME REGION LOIRE VALLEY, FRANCE
This is home to those famous Sauvignon Blanc-growing villages of Pouilly-Fumé and Sancerre, which, as you might recognize, also give their names to the wine style. These wines are known for being delicate and zesty, with herbaceous flavours and minerality. They're a hugely popular choice on wine lists because they have such a good reputation, and although they're exquisite, they can sometimes be overpriced. If you want a

decent Loire Sauvignon without the price tag of the famous villages, try a Sauvignon de Touraine.

BORDEAUX, FRANCE

Sauvignon Blanc has two jobs in Bordeaux. Firstly, it's used to make a zesty, dry wine. Sometimes it is used on its own to do this, but it's more common to find it blended with Semillon. These dry whites are usually crisp, citrus-fresh and herbaceous, similar to the ones in the Loire Valley, but generally a bit chewier in the mouth. Secondly, it is used to make sweet wines. Again, these are usually blended with Semillon, and sometimes with another white grape called Muscadelle. The wines are honeyed, with a delicious marmalade and candied orange flavour. Famous regions (and again, style names) are Sauternes and Barsac.

NEW ZEALAND

This is where the new generation of Sauvignon Blanc began, and these wines historically reek of tropical fruits like passion fruit, mango and pineapple; sometimes, they even smell of sweat. Today though, they can be far more elegant, too. Marlborough is the South Island region where this country's Sauvignon Blanc hype began, and largely thanks to one producer, Cloudy Bay.

Today, Sauvignon Blanc is a signature wine for all of the country's winemaking regions, although Marlborough is still thought of as the epicentre. There are almost too many good producers to choose from, but among my favourites outside of Marlborough are Craggy Range

Did you Know?

Sauvignon Blanc falls under the umbrella term 'aromatics' for pungent grapes, and is a parent to the red grape Cabernet Sauvignon (see pages 34-41). It also loves to be blended with Semillon, especially in the production of sweet wines (see pages 104-109 and 164-169).

and Neudorf. In Marlborough itself, I'm a fan of Seresin, Te Whare Ra and Dog Point. Cloudy Bay is famous for putting NZ wine on the map, but it also makes a lovely oaky version of Sauvignon Blanc called Te Koko, and this is the style that is becoming more popular, too.

USA

America has made a serious contribution to the Sauvignon Blanc world stage – putting it in contact with oak barrels (see page 55). This style usually goes by the name of Fumé Blanc and is most often found in the USA. However, and although it's still pretty niche, it's a growing trend around the world.

While this style can be a real success, it can dumb down the vibrancy of flavours in Sauvignon Blanc. They often have a smoky, earthy character as the wood deliberately calms down the full-on fruitiness of the wine, but also makes the wine incredibly food-friendly. Some of the best producers of this style include Robert Mondavi and Ferrari-Carano, both in California.

CHILE

Improving in quality all the time, Chile can make fantastic Sauvignon Blanc. When looking for the best that Chile has to offer, look out for regions that are close to the sea, like Casablanca, which is the traditional white wine Mecca for top-quality Chilean white wines. One of the most exciting things about the Chilean wine scene at the moment is the new regions, like Limari Valley and a tiny little area called Paradones. Both of these regions make juicy Sauvignon Blancs, but with a zesty grapefruit freshness and a salty tang, because their vineyards are surrounded by sea air. There are loads

Trends

These days, some Loire producers are trying to emulate the New Zealand Sauvignon by making more tropical-flavoured wines and putting Kiwi-related images and wording on the label.

of great examples, but some of my favourites are Casa Silva Cool Coast and Undurraga Terroir Hunter.

SOUTH AFRICA

They might not thank me for this, but South African Sauvignon Blanc grapes make wines that are often described as halfway between the delicate Sauvignon from the Loire Valley and the tropical fruitiness of the southern hemisphere. Based on the wines I have tasted, I think that's a fair description. My favourite region? Elgin. And here, the producer Iona makes some very cool wines. That said, Durbanville is another region making crisp and cool South African Sauvignon Blanc.

AUSTRALIA

Sauvignon Blanc is made all over Australia, but it's best known when it's blended with Semillon (see pages 104–109). The region it's made in is crucial, because Sauvignon Blanc thrives in cooler spots. This means regions like Adelaide Hills in South Australia have the advantage over the country's hotter spots.

Making sweet wines

Sweet wines like Sauternes rely on the grapes being infected by a 'good' disease called Botrytis cinerea or 'noble rot'. This disease pierces the skins of the grapes, causing the water inside to evaporate, leaving behind a grape with a high sugar concentration.

Organic, biodynamic, natural

What's an organic wine?

Organic wine today means that everything from grape-growing to bottling the final wine is done organically, which includes rules such as the banning of synthetic chemical fertilizers, pesticides and herbicides in the vineyard, and capping the amount of sulphur that's used as a preservative. After three years of proven organic practice, wine producers can apply for organic certification from official bodies such as ECOCERT. The term 'organic wine' only came into being in 2012. Before that, wines could only be described as being made 'from organically-grown grapes'.

Where do organic wines come from?

Grapes with the best chance of organic success are in warm and dry climates because there's less chance of disease, and therefore fewer chemical treatments are needed for the grapes to survive.

Can a wine be organic and not certified?

Yes. Many producers adhere to organic wine practices without seeking accreditation from an official body.

What's the difference between biodynamic and organic?

People often confuse the two, because the French word for organic wine is the widely used term 'bio' (short for *biologique*), while biodynamic is *biodynamie*.

Anyway, being biodynamic is totally different to being organic because it's more spiritual, that's to say the people who follow it have a belief in a philosophy rather than think of it as a practice to be followed. Biodynamic producers make their wines with respect to the environment, so the whole production system is healthy and harmonious for the environment. Most famously, this includes respecting the different influences of the cosmos on growing conditions. For example, the position of the moon and the stars has a bearing on when and if certain procedures happen; so do the time of the year and the time of the day.

Producers with a proven biodynamic record can also get certification – one official certifier is DEMETER.

What's a natural wine?

Natural wine has captured the zeitgeist of the last decade because of a belief (by some) that the modern wine world has become increasingly homogenized. The people who make natural wines believe wine is 'cleaned up' so much in the production process that wines around the world have become indistinguishable.

There's no set definition of a natural wine, though, and everyone has their own opinion on what it should be. It's a holistic approach, so the levels of 'naturalness' can vary from producer to producer. Essentially, though, it means a wine that's made with as little interference as possible – this includes using natural yeasts and organically-grown grapes. Sulphur is one of the key issues in the natural wine debate, because without sulphur, wines generally have a shorter shelf life; they oxidize more quickly, which can change their colour, and sometimes lead to a vinegary aroma.

What are Fairtrade® wines?

The Fairtrade® initiative involves local sustainability and the production of products made by people in the developing world who are provided with decent working conditions, all in an effort to improve their quality of life. It also includes fair terms of trade, so prices must never fall lower than the market price.

CHENIN BLANC

chewy • creamy •
dry • fresh • rich •
sweet • waxy

SMELLS
floral • herbaceous
oaky

TASTES OF
apple • apricot •
biscuit/cookie •
butter • honey •
lemon • melon •
mushroom • nuts •
peach • pear

If you're new to wine, chances are Chenin Blanc isn't going to blow your mind. I say this because when I show Chenin Blanc to people, I often get this 'so what?' look in return. But persevere with it, please, because this is a classic case of not judging a book by its cover.

Chenin Blanc is a complex grape and can make a complex wine. It's a bit like Chardonnay on the face of things, in the sense that it's relatively neutral. It hasn't got the wham-bam-thank-you-ma'am aroma satisfaction of, say, a Sauvignon Blanc; instead it's quiet and reserved, and takes time to open out.

Chenin Blanc is made into all styles of wine: still and sparkling, dry, off-dry and full-on sweet wines, although most of its flavour typically comes from one or a combination of three things – age, oak and lees. Older vintages of good Chenin Blanc can be gorgeous, and it has the capacity to age for a long time, too – I'm talking decades, so seek out older styles if you can. As with Chardonnay, when Chenin Blanc has spent time in contact with oak, it takes on a nutty flavour and chewy texture. Usually, this will boost its food-friendly credentials. Lees are the yeast deposits left after fermentation, and it's very common practice to let a Chenin Blanc 'sit' on the lees after the wine has been made. When this happens, the wine soaks up more yeasty flavour and, just like with the oak, can give an extra chewiness and richness to the wine.

So how does it taste? Well, Chenin Blanc can be chirpy and zesty in the first flush of youth, nutty and waxy if it's a bit older or has some oak on it, or can be a gorgeous, sticky, unctuous mouthful of marmalade and orange when it's sweet.

REGIONS & FLAVOURS

HOME REGION LOIRE VALLEY, FRANCE

If this were a book with sound effects, this chapter would sound like a long, deep and satisfied sigh because Chenin Blanc can make some truly hedonistic white wines from here, whether dry or sweet. Wines that are from the Loire villages of Vouvray, Quarts de Chaume, Bonnezeaux and Montlouis make delicious sweet versions of Chenin Blanc. The grapes for these wines are picked late off the vine, which means they have a high concentration of sugar. For medium-sweet Chenin Blanc, the region of Vouvray is perhaps the most famous village (and style) – it's deliciously fruity, and not sickly at all, while Savennières is the region that really champions bone-dry Chenin Blanc. Some of my favourite Chenin Blanc producers in the Loire include Domaine Huet and Nicolas Joly.

SOUTH AFRICA

Chenin Blanc is South Africa's flagship white grape and there's twice as much Chenin Blanc planted here as there is in the Loire, which only goes to show just how seriously this country takes this grape. Like in France, it's used for everything from dry to sweet and rocks up all over the country. One of the reasons it does well here is that there's a good supply of old Chenin Blanc vines, which are said to add complexity in the grapes and, subsequently, the wine. These wines can be complex, nutty and full of honeyed flavours. The best ones carry all of these things, but are zingy and fresh, too. One of the most exciting white wine developments for me in the last few years happened in Cape

Town, in 2012. You might call it an epiphany, and it began when I tasted a beautiful white blend called Cartology, made by Chris Alheit. It tasted of lemon peel and ripe apple, but it was also savoury and earthy. This wine was just the beginning of an adventure of gorgeous white blends I tasted during that trip, and I've been an avid fan ever since.

These white blended wines are often based on Chenin Blanc, with smaller amounts of other grapes added in, sometimes made up of five or six grapes, sometimes a lot more; and I think we're at the beginning of seeing this trend develop further, or at least I hope we are.

Some of my favourite Chenin Blanc producers, whether it's straight Chenins or blends include Chris Alheit, Mullineux, Sadie Family and Adi Badenhorstr.

USA

There are smatterings of Chenin Blanc to be found across the USA. In California though, especially in the Central Valley, Chenin Blanc has a bit of a tainted reputation because massive yields of the grape leave it with little flavour, and so a lot of this kind of Chenin Blanc is blended away with a white grape (that isn't particularly illustrious) called Colombard. Made this way, you can see why people don't get very excited about it. But that's not to say there aren't a few highlights in this state, the region of Clarksburg in the Sacramento Delta is doing a decent job at showing Chenin Blanc's true potential, while in Sonoma, try the Chenin Blanc from Dry Creek Vineyard. Meanwhile, on the east coast, Paumanok Vineyards on Long Island is known for its cult Chenin Blanc following.

Also Known as...

Chenin Blanc has synonyms – it's sometimes called 'Anjou' in the Loire Valley or 'Steen' in South Africa, which is the Dutch word for 'stone'. Whatever it's called, Chenin Blanc is the darling of the funky new white blends coming out of South Africa, especially from the region of Swartland.

Further enlightenment...

Want to know about oak's influence on a wine's flavour? See pages 54–55. Want to know about fizz made from Chenin Blanc? See pages 173–176.

SEMILLON

CHARACTERISTICS
fresh • dry • succulent • creamy waxy • sweet • luscious

SMELLS
grassy • herbaceous • tropical • zesty

TASTES OF
apple • dried fruit • grapefruit • honey • lemon • lime • nuts

Semillon is one of those grapes that does more than most people realize. In Bordeaux, its influence is massive, because not only is it a crucial blending partner with Sauvignon Blanc to make dry white wines, but it's also one of the key grapes in the sexy sweet wines of Sauternes and Barsac.

Why do they work so well together? Because Semillon and Sauvignon Blanc have a yin-yang relationship. Sauvignon Blanc can seem austere and uptight to some people, but when you throw the fatter, oilier Semillon into the mix, the tension in Sauvignon Blanc relaxes; you can almost hear it breathe a sigh of relief. Ultimately, this combination makes a fruity and well-rounded wine.

Semillon doesn't always need Sauvignon Blanc, though. It works on its own, too, although it doesn't have masses of natural flavour. When it's made for very early drinking it can be grassy and zesty, and when it's ripe, it will be full and round. Some of the most delectable dry Semillons I've ever tasted have come from Australia once they've been aged a good seven or eight years – this is when they taste of almonds and baked apples, and have a deep golden colour. Semillon is found all over the world these days, but the places that champion it most are Bordeaux and Australia.

REGIONS & FLAVOURS

HOME REGION BORDEAUX, FRANCE

As I mentioned on the previous page, the relationship between Sauvignon Blanc and Semillon works a dream in Bordeaux, where they're made into dry, light wines that are made to be drunk when the wines are young, nippy and zesty. In Sauternes and Barsac, Semillon is a crucial component in making the honeyed, candied fruit and unctuous sweet wines of these regions (and wine styles with the same name). When Semillon is crafted into this style of wine, it can age for much longer than a dry version of the wine would.

AUSTRALIA

Australia has really taken Semillon under its wing in a region in New South Wales called Hunter Valley (sometimes just shortened to 'Hunter'), which makes gorgeous wines from pure Semillon.

The vines here are very old, too, and, like with Chenin Blanc in South Africa, older vines are thought to add increased complexity to the wine. Hunter Semillons that are eight to 10 years old have a gorgeous waxy, biscuity/cookie character, while they're smooth and supple on the palate. They are real wines to savour. Tyrrell's Vat 1 Hunter Semillon is always sold a little bit older than other white wines and is a classic of this great Australian style, other great producers here include Brokenwood and Mount Pleasant.

Hunter Valley isn't the only place to find lush Australian Semillon, though. It's also made into a polished white wine in the Clare Valley and Margaret River area in Western Australia.

Meet Muscadelle

One of Semillon's most important roles in the world of wine is as a sweet wine, but Muscadelle is a French grape that often pops up in the same places as Semillon. Its best contribution is to making sweet wines, partly because Muscadelle has a very thin skin. When a grape has a thin skin, it's more susceptible to disease, and one of the 'good' grape diseases, Botrytis cinerea, is responsible for making some of the most mind-blowing sweet wines in the world (see page 92), so step forward Muscadelle. Yes, Muscadelle is sometimes used with Sauvignon Blanc and Semillon to make those sticky Bordeaux wines of Sauternes and Barsac. However, it's more used - and more famous in a region not too far from Bordeaux, Bergerac, for one sweet wine in particular: the gorgeous marmalade-flavoured Monbazillac. Muscadelle also crops up in Australia, which, as we know, is important for Semillon, too. Like in France, it makes both dry and sweet wines, but the best ones by far are those sweet wines made in Rutherglen, Victoria, in Australia. Here, producers often call it 'Rutherglen Topaque'. Topaque used to be known as 'Tokay', because they thought the grape originally came from Tokaj in Hungary. Give the Rutherglen Topaques from Stanton & Killeen or Campbells a go, they are heaven in a glass.

Château de Monbazillac, Dordogne, France

VIOGNIER

Say it:
vee-on-ee-yay

CHARACTERISTICS
pungent • juicy •
exotic • creamy •
perfumed •
luscious

SMELLS
floral • spicy

TASTES OF
apricot • caramel •
dried fruit • honey
mango • peach •
pineapple •
vanilla

A red grape masquerading as a white grape: that's how I once heard Viognier described. What a brilliant description. Viognier has attitude and oomph, and guts and texture, and it likes being blended into red wines. It's a red grape in all but colour.

I have a soft spot for Viognier because its flavour is very distinguishable. It's all about the peachy fruit, and when it's really good, beneath this luscious fruit there'll be extra layers of flavour: apricot, vanilla, honey and almond. Viognier isn't just used to make a fruity white wine either. It's also hugely important for pepping up the aroma and freshness in wines made from the red Syrah grape in the Rhône Valley. But that's not exclusive to France – you can find producers doing this in Australia, South Africa and the USA, too. Viognier is so pungent, you don't even need a large amount added into a red wine to make itself known; even the slightest of Viognier drops are noticeable when blended with Syrah/Shiraz. Viognier is also happy being blended with white grapes, and especially with other white grapes grown in the Rhône Valley, like Marsanne and Roussanne. Since around the millennium, Viognier has enjoyed a new lease of life, thanks to producers in Australia and California too, because before then, it only existed in very small quantities in France.

REGIONS & FLAVOURS

HOME REGION RHÔNE VALLEY, FRANCE

It's mind-blowing to think that before 2000, Viognier barely existed outside of this region. Here in its motherland, Viognier has two important roles. It can make a soft, peach-flavoured white wine and it's the grape behind one of the rarest white wines in the world – Condrieu. Its other role is to act as an aroma- and flavour-enhancer for red Syrah/Shiraz, especially in the Rhône sub-region of Côte-Rôtie.

CALIFORNIA

One of California's most successful white grapes, the juice factor in Viognier from California is off the charts. It can be so intense, it's almost like sniffing, and drinking, a can of peaches in syrup. Cline Cellars in Sonoma produces some delicious full-flavoured examples with classic aromas of peach, apricot and honey.

AUSTRALIA

In certain patches of Australia, Viognier has thrived in adversity, even though it's a tricky variety to grow. This is because it takes a long time to ripen, but if it's too ripe it loses its freshness extremely quickly. Both on its own as a white wine (where the outcome is usually somewhere between the juiciness of California and the elegance of the Rhône) and as an addition to red wine, Viognier's worth is demonstrated by the fact that many of Australia's top Shiraz producers add a splash of it to their very best wines.

Naming Viognier

Condrieu is one of the most expensive Viognier wines in the world. This is the name of a wine-producing region in the northern Rhône Valley, as well as the wine style made from the Viognier grape.

Yalumba is an Australian producer that has gone to great pains to put Viognier back on the map, and its Viognier is one of the best around. It comes from the southern Australian region, Eden Valley, and is full-bodied, floral and silky-smooth.

SOUTH AFRICA

Maybe it's unfair to say that Viognier is hugely important to South Africa's white wine scene by default, because Syrah/Shiraz is also really important to South Africa, but the fact is, it is important because of this. Many a South African Syrah/Shiraz has Viognier in the mix, à la Rhône. That said, there are some good white Viogniers to be had, too, especially when mixed into gorgeous white wine blends with Chenin Blanc (see pages 98–103), but also on their own. I especially like the varietal (single grape) style made by The Foundry in Stellenbosch.

SOUTHERN FRANCE

The Rhône Valley and the south of France often share grape varieties, so it's no surprise to learn that Viognier can be found in Languedoc-Roussillon, just not in vast quantities. These Viogniers are full of fleshy peach fruit but are not as pungent as those from the New World. And what's more, they're often more affordable than those from the Rhône.

NEW ZEALAND

In the race to prove itself as more than a one-trick white wine pony (Sauvignon Blanc), other grapes in the catch-all group 'aromatics' include Viognier, which is proving to be successful here, again albeit in small volumes and both as a white wine and as a blend with some of its Syrah/Shiraz, which is especially good in the region of Hawke's Bay. I've also tasted some lovely, fresh Viogniers from Marlborough, the land of Sauvignon Blanc, made by a producer called Churton.

Esk Valley vineyard, Hawke's Bay, New Zealand

MUSCAT

perfumed • dry •
light • exotic •
fresh • sweet •
luscious

SMELLS
floral • perfumed

TASTES OF
apple • apricot •
grape • ginger •
lemon • orange •
pear • sultana/
golden raisin

Muscat is a grape which, for once, actually smells and tastes like a grape. It often confuses people, though, because its name changes frequently, depending on the country of origin (Moscatel in Spain and Portugal, Moscato in Italy, Moschato in Greece) and because it can be, and is, made into a still or sparkling, dry or sweet, and a table or fortified wine. Because of this, I look at this grape according to style rather than region, just to make things really clear.

Muscat is also a grape that mutates very easily, so there are tons of variations of it, so this section is dedicated to the highest-quality one, Muscat Blanc à Petits Grains. Although it doesn't make a dry, light wine very often, it's a useful little grape for pepping up the aroma and flavour in wines that are more neutral.

Muscat Blanc à Petits Grains grows all across France in different varieties from different regions that are included in the names of the grapes – Muscat de Frontignan, Muscat d'Alsace, Muscat de Beaumes-de-Venise – as well as all over Piedmont in Italy. Other Muscat classifications include Muscat Ottonel and Muscat d'Alexandrie, which are slightly inferior to the Muscat Blanc à Petits Grains I look at here. Muscat is an ancient grape variety and because it's so old there's constant discussion over where its true 'home' lies. For Muscat Blanc à Petits Grains, many people believe the answer is Greece, from where it's thought to have spread across Europe. Over the years, this grape has mutated so much, it's possible to find versions of this grape that are pink and black as well as its best known colour, white.

REGIONS & FLAVOURS

DRY OR SLIGHTLY SWEET
ALSACE, FRANCE
Muscat is one of the key white grapes grown in Alsace and makes cute, light wines. They are delicate, classically grapey in flavour and pair well with Asian dishes, especially when lemongrass is the main ingredient. Charles Schléret and Hugel both make delicious dry Muscats. Alsace makes sweet wines, too, of course, but these are not generally made from Muscat. The sweeter ones will say Vendange Tardive (VT) or Sélection de Grains Nobles (SGN) on the label.

SLIGHTLY SWEET & SPARKLING
ITALY
Moscato is usually found in the north of Italy — it's the most planted white grape in Piedmont because it's used to make the sparkling wines Asti and the superior Moscato d'Asti.

Moscato d'Asti
This is a moreish, delicate and underrated wine — it's my go-to wine as a lighter style of dessert wine. It isn't as sparkling or as high in alcohol as Asti. Moscato d'Asti has a pretty elderflower taste, which, combined with its gentle spritz and low alcohol (usually around 5% ABV — alcohol by volume), makes it a great wine to finish off a meal with, because you have a little hit of sweetness without any of the richness that can come from typical sweet wines. Vajra, Elio Perrone and Poderi Einaudi all make delicious Moscato d'Astis.

RHÔNE VALLEY, FRANCE

Clairette de Die is a neat little sparkling wine that's mostly made from Muscat (a minimum of 75%). It's another pretty, lightly fizzy wine that tastes of honey and honeysuckle, and has around 7% ABV.

SWEET
ROUSSILLON, FRANCE

Muscat de Rivesaltes is the name given to a *vin doux naturel* (fortified sweet wine) made here in the south of France. These are full-on sweet wines and can carry higher alcohol levels too (sometimes 16–17% ABV). When young, they taste of apricots and tropical fruits, and when older, they take on a nutty, orange flavour. This style is made with a proportion of Muscat Blanc à Petits Grains together with Muscat d'Alexandrie.

SWEET & FORTIFIED
AUSTRALIA

Liqueur Muscat is a gorgeous and ancient-tasting fortified wine made in the state of Victoria – the area of Rutherglen considers it a speciality, and often it's referred to as Rutherglen Muscat. These Muscats are sweet and complex, and are aged for long periods in wood, where they become incredibly intense wines that smell of tobacco and wood, and taste of caramel and treacle/molasses.

GREECE

Most sweet Greek Moschatos are *vin doux naturels*. Sweet Greek Moschatos are usually a dark-orange or amber colour, and many of the Greek islands make a version of this wine, although those made on the

Vin doux naturel

Vin doux naturel is a fortified sweet wine whose alcohol fermentation is stopped deliberately early. This means it has a high level of sugar, leaving the wine sweet.

Gewürztraminer *Say it: guh-vertztra-meener*

Muscat and Gewürztraminer are both famous for having an incredibly strong perfume. Found across northern Europe, Gewürz (as it's often called) is increasingly turning up in New World countries such as New Zealand, Australia and Chile. It makes both a dry and sweet wine, and is found by itself as well as blended with other grapes. Its typical characters are rose, lychee and ginger so it's commonly used to pep up the aroma of a more subtle grape. Gewürz is happiest when grown in cooler climates, both to preserve this special perfume and because it's a grape that can reach high levels of sugar (and therefore alcohol).

island of Samos are especially famous and good. The local cooperative in Samos makes most of the wines on the island. They taste of toffee, nuts and marmalade, and are deliciously unctuous. The flavours last a long time on the palate and they're delicious with a slice of orange cake.

RIESLING

Say it: reeze-ling

CHARACTERISTICS
dry • perfumed •
vibrant • fresh •
exotic • elegant •
delicate • sweet •
luscious

SMELLS
floral • grass •
herbaceous •
perfumed • of
petrol/gasoline

TASTES OF
elderflower •
ginger • green
apple • honey •
lemon • lime •
mango • orange •
passion fruit •
peach • pineapple

Don't turn the page! Look, I know Riesling can be a massive no-no for some people, but one of the sad truths about this delicious grape is that when people don't realize they're drinking Riesling they actually love it. And so they should, because Riesling makes some of the classiest white wines in the world, and for this reason it's really respected by those in-the-know.

Despite this, it still suffers from two major misconceptions: people think it's low-quality or sweet. Some people think it's both, so let's take a closer look at these accusations.

'Riesling is low-quality.' This stems from the days of Liebfraumilch, that cheap, sugar-water German wine that had its heyday in the 1960s and '70s. But the truth is that Liebfraumilch wasn't even Riesling most of the time! But yes, Riesling is Germany's signature grape and it makes some of the purest, most complex white wines in the world.

'All Riesling is sweet.' So much Riesling is dry. Like, bone-dry. Yes, it can be hard to determine what is and isn't sweet sometimes, and if more wine bottles adopted the international sweetness scale on the back of their labels, our lives, and Riesling's life, would be much easier. Yes, there are sweet Rieslings to be found, but what's wrong with that anyway? They can be some of the most remarkable wines in the world.

Still unconvinced? Then just try Riesling with food. It's an incredible food-pairing wine, especially with Asian dishes, plus it's often low in alcohol. And finally, it's super-fruity, which is why so many people love it when they taste it anonymously. Riesling is also great at retaining its identity from place to place, so it can be more difficult to distinguish one region from another than with other grapes.

REGIONS & FLAVOURS

HOME REGION GERMANY

German Riesling can taste like one of the purest wines in the world. The best can age really well, partly because their high acidity gives them the ability to age. When this happens, they can turn from wines packed with elderflower and floral aromas, full of lemon and lime flavours when young, to having a rich, honeyed and kerosene flavour. One of the most famous regions is Mosel, and Rieslings from here are pretty, delicate and have an elderflower purity with zingy freshness. This region has such a cool climate that the slightly sweeter style of Riesling works really well at softening the crisp acidity.

ALSACE, FRANCE

Alsace is the main French region for Riesling and the go-to place for dry, food-friendly wines, because Alsace Riesling is often dry, and when it's super-sweet, you'll find the words 'Vendange Tardive' (VT) or 'Sélections de Grains Nobles' (SGN) on the label. Grand Cru wines have come from the best vineyards.

How sweet?

Want to know the sweetness levels on German Riesling? Look for the international Riesling scale on the back of bottles. (See pages 14-15 'Label logic' for more.)

Generally, Rieslings from Alsace don't have the full-on, pungent aroma that you find in Germany, but they are still very serious wines, and seriously elegant, too. Some of my favourite producers are Domaine Weinbach, Albert Mann and Humbrecht.

AUSTRIA

In Austria, Riesling plays second fiddle to native grape Grüner Veltliner, but it shouldn't be ignored as it cuts a really nice halfway house between the fruitiness of German Riesling and the texture and weight in the mouth of those you get in Alsace. Austria's most famous region is Wachau, where hot days and cool nights help to make the Riesling grapes smell especially fragrant. The Wachau Rieslings from Weingut Knoll and Weingut Prager are gorgeous.

USA

Both the East Coast and West Coast of North America are loving Riesling these days. The Washington State sub-region, Columbia Valley, feels like the spiritual home of Riesling in the USA – it's also home to the world's largest Riesling producer, Chateau Ste Michelle. This estate, together with German Riesling supremo Ernie Loosen, makes a delicious Riesling called Eroica.

On the East Coast, it's the Finger Lakes region in New York that's making waves with Riesling. The harsh conditions here can be painfully cold, but it means hardy Riesling thrives in most years, although some years it can even be too cold for Riesling. These often dry wines are not as aromatic as others, but they are more generous than European Rieslings in the mouth. Think of them as European Riesling without ice cubes – these are rounder and fruitier. Dr Konstantin Frank makes some lovely wines here; so, too, does Hermann J. Wiemer.

AUSTRALIA

Australian Riesling are the most distinctive Riesling in my mind, because of their strong lime character. They are über-crisp, clear and pure, but also have an exotic twist. The best regions are in South Australia; Clare Valley and Eden Valley. Cool winds at night keep the

Riesling from becoming too big and blowsy. Grosset, Pewsey Vale and Clos Clare make some gorgeous versions of zesty, floral, dry Riesling.

NEW ZEALAND

There are Riesling highlights throughout the country, but my go-to regions are all in the South Island. The most famous is the Waipara Valley, and Riesling here ranges from being German in style, with pure fruit, to Alsace in style, when it is more minerally. But be warned: the sweetness levels here can vary, although they're pretty good at declaring the sweetness on the label. Spy Valley and Pegasus Bay wines are lovely. Then there's Marlborough, check out Te Whare Ra's Riesling – delicious. It's also the main white grape in Central Otago, which has plenty of vineyards on schist soils, perfect for Riesling. Peregrine and Prophet's Rock make zingy, dry Rieslings here.

Vineyards in Mosel valley, Loesnich, Germany

PINOT GRIGIO/PINOT GRIS

CHARACTERISTICS
perfumed · fresh ·
chewy · buttery ·
light · subtle

SMELLS
floral · grassy ·
herbaceous · of
pear · perfumed

TASTES OF
apple · apricot ·
citrus · grapefruit ·
honey · lemon ·
nuts · pear · pear
drops/hard candy

It's hard to be honest about Pinot Grigio without sounding like a complete snob, but the truth is that Pinot Grigio is a lot more famous for being fashionable than for being a complex wine. But maybe that's part of its appeal; a friend once told me she liked Pinot Grigio because it tasted of nothing!

I totally understand why people get confused between Pinot Grigio and its alter ego, Pinot Gris. I mean, it is the same grape, but there's usually a world of difference in the taste and complexity, because when wines are labelled Pinot Gris, they generally have a deeper, richer flavour. New World producers will produce both Pinot Grigio and Pinot Gris, each with its own distinct style according to the name.

But back to Pinot Grigio for a moment. It's a grape that has taken the world by storm in the last decade or so. It makes a light, crisp white that tastes of pear drops/hard candy, and because of its immense popularity has gone ballistic; every winemaking country is cashing in on it, from Australia to Argentina.

REGIONS & FLAVOURS

HOME REGION FRANCE
Pinot Gris, we *think*, started out in Burgundy,

because it's actually a version of Pinot Noir that became white over the years. But not many people today think of it that way, now that Pinot Grigio – its Italian incarnation – is so ubiquitous. So today, it's rare to find Pinot Gris in Burgundy, where it's sometimes called 'Pinot Beurot'; but thanks to an ancient law, it's still permissible to use a tiny drop of Pinot Gris in red Burgundy, although I can't imagine this ever happens these days. The most famous French region for Pinot Gris is the north-eastern region of Alsace, where it makes both a sweet and dry wine, and generally has more guts and depth to it than the Italian Pinot Grigio.

VENETO, ITALY

This north-eastern region is home to the masses of Pinot Grigio that set the trend around the world. It's for early drinking, should be drunk very cold, and tastes of pear drops/hard candy, and grapefruit, too, if you're lucky. Its popularity has one advantage, though: it's made us sit up and take notice of Italian white wines in general (see page 134-137), even if Pinot Grigio is still by far the most popular. Take a look at those from Pasqua, Masi and È Solo.

FRIULI, ITALY

Of all the Pinot Grigio versions that now exist, my favourites hail from this little pocket of north-eastern Italy, where super-crisp white wines are made in general. Here, Pinot Grigio tends to have more concentration than that from the Veneto. The best ones I've tried have a really strong, lemon-peel concentration to the fruit flavours, even if they are still frisky, early-drinking wines. Try the dry, full-bodied

Grigio versus Gris

Grigio is usually reserved for wines that are pretty with sweet, floral aromas and are drunk very young. Gris is a richer-tasting version of the grape, with more waxy flavours, and is sometimes buttery, too. They can usually be enjoyed at an older age than most Grigio.

Grigios with their rich, floral and fruity aroma from Visintini and Jermann.

ALSACE, FRANCE

It's incredible to think how delicious Alsace Pinot Gris can be, as opposed to the lighter Pinot Grigios from around the world. Alsace makes textbook Pinot Gris with flavours of apples and nuts, and it can even taste round and buttery. Plus, it can age well. It's brilliantly food-friendly and subtle in style, but has many layers of flavour. Usually, it comes in one of those tall, flute-shaped bottles, but don't let that put you off (if you think these are for sweeter wines) – it's often dry in style. There's a bank of producers here that make excellent Pinot Gris, and I really rate Josmeyer, Hugel and Domaine Weinbach.

USA

Oregon and Washington State make Pinot Gris; that's to say they are more Alsace in style, with a chewy texture and a nutty flavour to add to the fruit. California hasn't missed a trick, either, with this über-popular grape, and it makes both Grigio and Gris.

NEW ZEALAND

Depending on the producer's whim, the styles here are either Grigio or Gris. But hopes are high in New Zealand that they can capitalize on people's love of the Pinot Grigio grape, especially because this country is so good at making the other 'aromatic' grapes, including its top dog, Sauvignon Blanc. Try the Grigio from Seifried or the Gris from Isabel Estate or Prophet's Rock.

The Aromatics family

Pinot Grigio is one of the white grapes that falls under the 'aromatics' umbrella, together with Sauvignon Blanc, Riesling and Gewürztraminer.

Hugel wine-tasting cellar rooms, Riquewihr, Alsace, France

ITALIAN WHITES

Pinot Grigio set the world alight at the beginning of the 21st century with its light and fruity style, opening the door for other Italian whites to follow. And, boy, did they follow! These are just a few of the very tasty Italian whites to look out for.

FALANGHINA
CENTRAL ITALY

A dry, nutty-flavoured wine with rich lemon fruit, we're seeing more of it on wine lists these days because it's crisp and usually quite ballsy for a white wine. This tastes at its best when it's young and fridge-cold.

FIANO & CARRICANTE
SICILY

Sicily's answer to fruity white wine comes from the local Fiano grape. It's easy to say, and easy to drink, because it can taste of lemons or apples. Carricante is one to watch and comes from the region around Mount Etna – it's chewy with ripe lemon and tangy orange flavours.

ARNEIS *Say it: arr-nay-iss*
PIEDMONT

With crisp, peachy fruit, a hint of almond, and sometimes a squeeze of orange, too, its home is in the Roero sub-region of Piedmont, and is often called 'Roero Arneis' on wine lists. It makes a delicious white wine with attitude and should be drunk young-ish.

PECORINO
MARCHE

This is an easy-drinking, mild-flavoured grape native to central Italy. Quality can vary, but overall I've found it to be crisp and always more complex than Pinot Grigio.

RIBOLLA GIALLA *Say it: ree-bolla jar-la*
FRIULI

Nutty and waxy in flavour and usually a deep-golden colour. This is a food white for me – the flavour is strong and it often has a chewy texture.

FRIULANO
FRIULI

Floral, juicy, pretty and perky, there's a lot to be said for a glass of chilled Friulano on a hot summer's day. Not much of it is made, but it's always been a winner in my book.

VERMENTINO
TUSCANY & SARDINIA

Thanks to Chianti, Tuscany is red wine country for most people. But the coast of Tuscany makes some blisteringly cool and crisp whites from the Vermentino grape (known as Rolle in the south of France). It's prolific in Sardinia, too; in fact, it's the signature white grape of this island. Salty, crisp and full of lemon flavour.

VERDICCHIO *Say it: vair-deek-ee-yo*
MARCHE

One of the better known of Italy's local grapes, Verdicchio is found all over Italy, but its most famous Italian home is in the region of Marche. Like many of its native Italian siblings, it's lemon-fresh and has that citrus and almond combination of flavour, although it's often accompanied by a crisp acid character.

GARGANEGA
VENETO & SICILY

If you haven't heard of the Garganega grape you've probably heard of one of its most famous wines, Soave. It's best known for having a delicate perfume, almond flavours and fresh acidity, but its production has suffered from quantity over quality over the years. Even so, the producer Pieropan makes attractive and serious wines using this grape.

Vineyards in Acquaviva Picena, Marche, Italy

SPANISH WHITES

There's much more to Spanish white wine than Albariño, as delicious as that can be. It's easy to think of Spain just as a hot country that's great for punchy reds, but it's a mountainous and coastal one, too, and these areas have cool enough conditions for perky white wines to be made as well. In fact, in the last 20 years or so, there's been a huge transformation in Spanish white wines, with a greater focus on zesty, fruity whites. The change in the Spanish white wine scene is (a bit like Italy's) thanks to an improvement in technology that has allowed producers to make the most of high-quality local grape varieties.

VERDEJO *Say it: ver-dec-koh*
RUEDA *Say it: roo-ay-dah*

Verdejo is one of the new darling white wines by-the-glass in restaurants and bars. It's most famously made in the northern Spanish region of Rueda, but it's also one of the most widely planted white grapes in the country. At its best it has a really intense aroma of flowers and nuts, especially almonds (almond is a common flavour note for many Spanish whites), while in the mouth it can be crisp but juicy. Sometimes it's blended with Sauvignon Blanc, and this makes it taste even more herbaceous. But you can also find oak-aged Verdejo, and when it's spent time in barrel, those nutty flavours really come into their own.

ALBARIÑO *Say it: al-bar-een-yo*
RÍAS BAIXAS *Say it: ree-as baish-as*

A perennially popular Spanish white grape that's known very well internationally, Albariño makes your quintessential coastal white wine, grown in Rías Baixas in Galicia, the coastal part of Spain that sits just above Portugal. It's in its element when paired with seafood. Albariño is all about a floral, zesty, citrus-flavoured white with a lick of sea-air saltiness, which is the secret to its fantastic match with fish and shellfish. These wines are made to be drunk young, while they're at their freshest, although there are always a few producers who are experimenting with different styles of 'classic' Albariño by using oak and mixing in other grape varieties that may help it age. Pazo de Señorans makes some seriously top-end Albariño, while Martín Códax's wines are also worth checking out.

GODELLO
VALDEORRAS

It's hard not to be seduced by the story of a grape on the verge of extinction being revived, and not just being revived, but also making delicious wine. North of the Portuguese border, the little-known region of Valdeorras has made big waves with Godello in the last 25 years. Today it makes very sunny wines full of fleshy peach flavours, but also with a cool and crisp edge to them. Godello has enough oomph and depth to stand up to time with oak (if that's the style producers want – a Godello with extra structure to age for a bit longer). If you're into luscious apple, nutty, developed flavours in your wine, give older Godello a try. Check out the wines of Rafael Palacios – these are nothing short of gorgeous.

VIURA
RIOJA

White Rioja's thunder is always stolen by red Rioja, which is a bit of a shame because the whites of this landlocked region of northern Spain can be very good. Like its red counterpart, white Rioja is usually made from a blend of grapes, except that in white Rioja, Viura is the star; with the red, it's the grape Tempranillo.

White Rioja has a traditional, loyal following, but I've got to admit that young white Rioja has never really set my heart racing, mostly because it doesn't seem to have as much flavour or personality as other Spanish whites. When young, it's fresh and crisp, but there's no overwhelming Viura flavour per se.

Some sommeliers, though, love a barrel-fermented Viura-based white Rioja because it can be very complex and have a waxy texture and flavour that is great for food. However, production of this style is on the decrease — it's become a casualty of Spain's white wine revolution because producers are concentrating on making light and zesty whites instead.

The producer Muga has a good reputation in Rioja and makes a good midway, everyday Viura-based white Rioja; it's been barrel-fermented but still tastes of melon fruit rather than wood. Typically, Viura is blended with Garnacha Blanca and Malvasia to make white Rioja, but I prefer Viura when it's used to make Cava, and it's actually one of the more popular grapes used in making Spain's leading sparkling wine. A common synonym for Viura is Macabeo, by the way.

GARNACHA BLANCA
ALL ACROSS SPAIN

Yes, Garnacha comes in white as well as red (and pink too, as it happens). Garnacha Blanca is found in various pockets of Spain, and most of those are in the north. Known as Grenache Blanc in France, it generally doesn't produce a wine that's going to rock the world by itself, as it isn't especially refined or classy. However, it does have its uses, especially in blended wines, where it can either boost the alcohol content or richen the body of a wimpy white.

One of Garnacha Blanca's most famous appearances is in white Rioja, although as I said before, Viura usually takes the lead role for white wines here.

Have you heard of Airén?

It's the most widely planted grape variety in Spain, although red grapes Tempranillo and Cabernet Sauvignon are now giving it a run for its money. That said, I wouldn't search too hard for a table wine made from this. It's mostly used in the production of Spanish brandy. Let's hope it stays that way!

HONDARRABI ZURI
CHACOLÍ/TXAKOLI *Say it: chak-oh-lee*

This one sounds a little bit crazy I know, that's because it's the local Basque name given to the most important grape in the region – and wine style – of Txakoli. Txakoli is also what you're more likely to see on the label, rather than this grape name.

Not much of it is made by Spanish winemaking standards, but its quality and production have improved considerably in the last 20 years. It makes crunchy white wines that taste of green apples and I love it for being incredibly fresh and zingy. The producer Txomín Etxaníz *(say it: cho-min etch-anith)* makes some lovely wines in this pretty Spanish spot. In French Basque country, this grape is known as Courbu Blanc.

MALVASIA
LANZAROTE

A few years ago, a Spanish sommelier friend of mine tipped the Canary Islands as a region to watch, and having since tasted some of the wines, I agree. Red wines probably rule here, but when Malvasia is done well it's really delicious, especially in Lanzarote, where the volcanic soils give a savoury, earthy edge to the apple-flavoured fruit.

MACABEO/XARELLO/PARELLADA (CAVA GRAPES)
PENEDÈS, CATALONIA

Cava is Spain's signature sparkling wine. It's a style name, though, rather than a region as most people think, and in fact can be made in a number of different Spanish locations. That said, the engine room of Cava is in Penedès in Catalonia, just west of Barcelona.

Cava has shared the limelight with Prosecco in recent years as the recessionary 'alternative' sparkling wine to Champagne because it's typically more affordable. But the Cava scene has been changing and the style is trying and succeeding in making more serious wines.

You can see this change in the grape varieties being used. Cava used to be made of very local Spanish grapes like Macabeo, Xarello and Parellada, and although these are still widely planted and used, the authorities have given winemakers permission to use Chardonnay and Pinot Noir in the wines. This has been significant in improving the quality of the traditionally appley-flavoured Cava, making some of it more complex and able to age.

Macabeo (Viura) I've talked about on a previous page, but as for the other two native Cava grapes, Xarello (sometimes spelt 'Xarel·lo' or 'Xarel-lo') is the most revered, and its reputation is better than that of Parellada because it has some oomph and guts to its flavour, together with a powerful freshness, which can be useful in the Spanish heat. For all the buzz about Chardonnay and Pinot Noir on today's Cava scene, some producers still prefer to stay very local, and one producer whose wines show the best of the local Xarello grape is Gramona, so track it down if you can. As for Parellada, this grape's most useful job in Cava is to make the wine smell floral.

Something different?

Palomino Fino and Pedro Ximénez are white Spanish grapes mostly used to make Sherry. But sometimes you can find them as dry table wines, too. They don't have as much character as some of the other white Spanish grapes, but they're an interesting and fresh alternative and definitely worth trying if you spot them.

ROSÉ

The world's love affair with pink shows no signs of
stopping and it's a versatile wine for all sorts of reasons.
Sure, it can be blush and sweet or a dry and quaffable
summery drink, but plenty have enough character and
personality to match well with food, and quite a wide
range of dishes too, including spicier ones.

Rosés can be made anywhere that red wines are made, because the colour comes from the skin of red grapes. The pulp (and therefore juice) of all grapes is colourless, which explains why you can make white wines from red grapes, as long as you separate the skins quickly enough. The colour of the pink varies hugely, from pale to Spanish onion-skin (as people in the wine trade say) to the colour of pomegranate seeds. The differences in colour depend on the grapes used and the length of maceration time (see below).

There are three ways to add colour to rosé: maceration, saignée and blending. Maceration keeps the pulp (juice) of the grape in contact with the skin of the grape, so it draws out colour. The longer this takes place, the darker the wine colour. Saignée is French for 'bled', and as a red wine starts to ferment, some of the wine will be 'bled' off into another container so the contact of the juice with the skins is shorter, making the wine pink rather than red. This method generally makes rich rosés. Finally, blending involves adding a little red wine to white wine. This is illegal in many places and is most widely done in Champagne, where it is legal.

DRY & ELEGANT
PROVENCE, FRANCE

Ahh... the engine room of some of the world's most delicious rosés. This is as serious as rosé can get, and local varieties, such as Syrah, Grenache, Carignan and Cinsaut, are to thank for the melting pot of tasty rosés from Provence. They're refreshing and bursting with floral, sweet, red apple and crunchy pomegranate fruit flavours, so they're a match made in heaven with the garlic and aioli-influenced food of the region. If you want to go swanky and serious, try Domaine Ott, and if you want something a bit more affordable and organic, too, Château Léoube is a great producer, but I'm also a fan of the wines at Domaine Sainte Lucie, which has a great brand called MiP (Made in Provence).

DRY OR OFF-DRY & ELEGANT
LOIRE VALLEY, FRANCE

There are some lovely, pretty rosés from the Loire Valley, usually made from Cabernet Franc or Pinot Noir. They're delicate, zesty and can sometimes have a little hit of extra sweetness, so small that you'd hardly notice, but enough to make them a great match with a dish that has some spice to it.

DRY OR OFF-DRY & FRUITY
PORTUGAL

Some of my favourite rosés, or *rosados* as the Portuguese say, come from Portugal. This country's local dark-skinned grapes have an abundance of natural flavour and colour, so it only stands to reason they'd work well as pink wines, too. In the Douro Valley, Touriga Nacional — which is the most famous grape in Port production — makes brilliant dry and perky pink wines. They often taste of pomegranate to me, although the best styles also have a sour, red grapefruit freshness. Speaking of Port, even that has got in on the rosé action now. Pink Port was created by the Port house, Taylor's, in 2010, and is so successful many other houses now make it, too. It's especially good as a base for cocktails. Other Portuguese rosado regions worth looking out for are Vinho Verde and Alentejo.

DRY OR OFF-DRY, FRUITY & SPICY
SOUTH OF THE EQUATOR

Generous sunshine hours make red grapes ripen easily, so countries like Chile, Argentina, South Africa, New Zealand and Australia can make some belter rosés, full of crunchy red fruits. They're sunshine in the bottle, and are made to be drunk in the sun, too! Typically, they're made with grapes that are best known within each country. In Chile, Cabernet Sauvignon, Merlot and Carmenère make deep-coloured rosés with lots of grip to the bright, juicy-fruit flavour. In Argentina, it's Malbec. The colour is deep and it tastes bold and fruity. In Australia, Shiraz and Cabernet Sauvignon make deep-coloured rosés with a good bite of black-pepper spice. Mostly dry, sometimes they're off-dry, too. In New

Zealand, the grape used varies by region. It could be Merlot, Pinot Noir or Syrah/Shiraz, but they're usually bright pink in colour, very fruity and dry. In South Africa, Pinotage rosés often have a smoky edge to their fruit, making them good for barbecues, and usually they're dry.

DRY, BOLD & FRUITY

NAVARRA, SPAIN

Many Spanish regions make *rosado*, of course, but Navarra is especially good for rich and handsome styles with bucket-loads of flavour and attitude. Usually, they're made from Garnacha and are deep pink in colour. Most of them are dry, and they have an upfront, juicy style with crushed-strawberry flavour.

PUGLIA, ITALY

Rosato, as the Italians call rosé, is made all over Italy, from the north-west corner of Piedmont to the heel in Puglia. Down in Puglia, in the sub-region of Salice Salentino, some lovely rosatos are made with plenty of rich colour, cherry-flavoured fruit and a zesty spice.

NAPA VALLEY, CALIFORNIA, USA

For drier rosés than the generic Californian style, take a look at those made in Napa with Cabernet Sauvignon. California's crown jewel of Cabernet Sauvignon production makes deep-coloured rosés with a richness of fruit that is so intense, if you tasted them blind you might even think you were drinking red wine.

You say rosé

Rosé is such a familiar wine name that it's universally used for pink wines, even if it isn't necessarily the right word in the wine's local language.

MEDIUM & FRUITY
CALIFORNIA, USA
Zinfandel Blush or White Zinfandel is a universally-loved wine style.
People love the sweeter style that tastes of confectionery, and these
wines are impossible to ignore on the shelf because the colour is
almost neon.

DRY & VERY LIGHT
FRIULI, ITALY
Check out Pinot Grigio Ramato if you like light rosé. Even though Pinot
Grigio is a white grape, it has a slight pink tinge to its skin, and
sometimes this comes through in the wine, giving a very light copper
colour that's enough to squeeze it into this rosé section. Pinot Grigio
Ramatos are very different to the Pinot Grigios most of us know, and
have a lightly chewy texture and a gentle apple flavour.

PINK FIZZ
Everywhere that makes sparkling wine usually makes a sparkling rosé,
too. These are typically fruitier versions of the white sparkling wines
from each region because the juice has spent more time leaking
flavour and colour from the red grapes. This means places such as
England, that have a cool climate, are especially proud of their
sparkling rosé wines because the red fruit gives them an extra layer of
flavour. Speaking of which, I really like the rosé from Gusbourne, and
Hush Heath. Rosé Champagnes also offer serious depth of flavour. I'm
a huge fan of those made by Charles Heidsieck, Bollinger and Dosnon
& Lepage.

ROSÉ & FOOD
I'm totally into dry rosé with food – it's really versatile so there are
many options.

Food coming off a griddle/grill pan has that extra-smoky flavour,
which means a robust (probably southern hemisphere) rosé is a great
option to pair with barbecue food. These should also have enough guts
to match the richness of, say, sausages, as well as enough freshness to

work with grilled/broiled sardines and salads. Spanish rosado is also delicious with these foods.

I especially like delicate and pretty rosés from Provence with the lightness-of-touch flavours inherent in Japanese food. Fruity rosés with depth of flavour and a hint of extra sugar, like those from the Loire, can go with subtly spicy dishes.

The versatility of rosé makes it a no-brainer picnic wine. While it's perky enough to work as an aperitif or with salads, the richer ones are great with charcuterie and goat's cheese, and the fruitier ones can also partner desserts. Try a Portuguese rosé.

Rosé is a catch-all option with most fish, but pink-fleshed fish and shellfish work especially well, whether it's salmon or prawns/shrimp, a dry rosé peps up these fishy flavours brilliantly. Try a dry Loire rosé or pink English fizz.

If sweet wine isn't your thing, then a punchy dry rosé can work well with dessert. If there are red fruits in the dessert, even better, because these have a natural affinity with the red-fruit flavours in the wines.

like it sweet?

If you prefer sweeter rosés, anything with the following phrases on the label will probably be sweeter: White Merlot, White Zinfandel, Zinfandel Blush or Pink Moscato.

Vineyard in Luberon area, Provence, France

FORTIFIED & SWEET

Dessert wines are the ultimate in luxurious indulgence and should be chosen with carefree abandon. At least that's how I like to think of them, because drinking them should feel like someone is wrapping you up in the softest cashmere blanket before giving you an enormous hug. Remember though, that fortified wines don't always fall into the dessert wine category, because those zingy, salty, sometimes nutty sherries can be as bone dry as table wine and drunk with savoury food.

FORTIFIED

What I really hope is that you're not just reading this page for one of these reasons: it's winter or Christmas, you want an after-dinner drink or you want a wine to go with dessert. Fortified wines are great for all these occasions, sure, but they also have a lot more to offer. They can be refreshing wines for any time of the year, many of them are gorgeous as an aperitif, and some can even pair their way through an entire meal. However, those people who freak out at the mention of fortified wine, or refuse even to let it pass their lips, usually act like this because: they think it's all sweet – it's not; they think it all tastes 'spirity' – it doesn't; or people get drunk after just one glass – they don't (although that depends on the size of the glass).

Fortified wine starts life in the winery like any normal table wine. Then it gets fortified. This involves adding a dollop of neutral-flavoured grape spirit to the wine, which doesn't change the flavour but does boost the alcohol level. Fortifying the wine is also the reason why many of them are sweet as well, because often the spirit is added to the wine before it's finished its conversion of sugar to alcohol (the fermentation process), and when there's a high level of leftover sugar in a wine, it's going to end up sweet.

Fortified wine is made all over the world, but there are three famous types: Port, Sherry and Madeira. We'll explore all of these here, as well as a few others that are lesser-known but are definitely worth drinking and knowing about. For the quality of the wine inside the bottle, fortified wines can be incredibly good value for money.

PORT
The name of Port is protected, so there's no such thing as 'Australian Port' or 'French Port', for example. It has to come from the Douro Valley in Portugal – one of the most beautiful wine regions in the world. Port can be white, pink or red, and most of it is sweet.

The Douro Valley is in northern Portugal, east of Oporto. Portugal is such a hotbed of native grapes, there can be as many as 80 different ones used in a red Port, but of these, here are the main and most common ones...

Touriga Nacional
This is the jewel in the Port crown and makes a wine with a concentrated and unique aroma, a deep colour and rich tannins.

Tinta Roriz
Also known as Tempranillo in Spain, this often gives a leathery flavour to the wine and can be high in alcohol with rich fruit flavour and tannins.

Touriga Franca
Popular for its floral aroma and deep colour, it's rich, but it's not as intense in flavour as one of its parents, Touriga Nacional.

Tinta Barroca
This can give a savoury, earthy flavour to the wine. It has very dark skins that make the wine very dark, too.

Tinta Cão
This is spicy and likes the cooler vineyard posts so it retains its lovely violet, floral aroma.

Port ranges in colour and is transformed into many different styles. The main ones, and their general characteristics are outlined here.

WHITE
This can be dry or sweet. It's made like a red Port, just using white grapes like Rabigato and Codega. White Port and tonic is a hugely popular long-drink aperitif in Portugal and is heavenly when served with toasted almonds.

PINK

A relatively new Port style, created by the Port house, Taylor's, but now made by several producers. This is an aperitif wine, really, and should be served chilled like White Port. It is also great in a summer cocktail (see page 201).

RUBY

The lightest and simplest style of red Port, it's sweet, made from a blend of different years and should be drunk as soon as it's bought, within two to three days once open.

TAWNY

A massively underrated wine, Tawny Port is aged for a long time in barrels. This contact with wood has made the Port turn a brown colour, hence the name. It's sweet and often tastes of oranges, nuts and toffee, and is delicious as a chilled aperitif or with desserts where orange, vanilla or nuts are key ingredients. Aged Tawny comes in a mix of years and you can gauge intensity by its average age on the label.

COLHEITA

This is a more intensely-flavoured version of Tawny Port, made from a single year.

VINTAGE

The pinnacle of Port production. Vintage Ports are only released in years the producers really rate. These are very serious wines that need

Declaring a Vintage Port

In the wine community, 'declaring' a vintage Port is a big deal. It happens when Port houses deem the year to be of exceptional quality, although each house can make this declaration independently. On average, a Vintage Port is declared about three times a decade.

to be stored laid down and are not for early drinking. They throw a sediment and therefore need decanting, and have an intense flavour that is mellow, rich, and full of fruit cake flavour that lasts for a long time.

LBV

'Late Bottled Vintage' is a great value-for-money wine and is especially good because it has all the richness and fruit of Vintage Port but without the hassle of decanting it. This is a Port that comes from one year, but it's spent more time in wood than Vintage Port, which softens it more quickly and therefore it can be drunk earlier. Although most LBV doesn't need decanting, if it says Traditional LBV on the label, it will.

SINGLE QUINTA

If a year's harvest is thought to be of very good quality but not quite good enough to declare it 'Vintage', then Port houses will make a wine from a particular plot (*quinta*) on their property. This is great as an after-dinner digestif – perfect for chocolate.

SHERRY

Like Port, the name of Sherry is protected. There's no such thing as an 'Italian Sherry' or a 'Californian Sherry', for example. It has to come from Andalucía in south-west Spain, and the word 'Sherry' is actually an English derivation of the place it comes from, Jerez. Sherry has been going through a popularity renaissance in recent years and it can be bone-dry or sweet and can range in colour from almost colourless to deep, opaque mahogany. For more on Sherry, see pages 162–163.

Palomino Fino

The most planted grape in the region of Jerez by a long way, Palomino Fino makes all of the dry sherries and is the base of many sherries that end up being sweet, too. By nature, it's a neutral-flavoured grape. The flavour you get in Sherry comes from its ageing process, not the grape's flavour.

Pedro Ximénez

This is usually referred to just by its initials: PX. On its own, it makes an intensely sweet wine that's an opaque brown colour, and tastes of liquorice and vanilla.

Moscatel

A grape commonly used to make sweet wines in Spain, it's only ever used to make a sweet Sherry, or, like with PX, to sweeten an existing dry Sherry (made with Palomino Fino).

The ageing process of Sherry in *bodegas* (the wineries where Sherry is made) is integral to how it tastes. There are two ways of ageing a Sherry; biologically and oxidatively. Biological ageing is for fino, manzanilla and amontillado. This involves a yeast layer called 'flor', forming on top of the wine in the barrel to stop contact with the air and limit oxidization so the wine stays fresh. This gives the Sherry a very yeasty, bready flavour. Fino and manzanilla are in the barrel for the shortest time, so they taste younger and are always dry. When the flor dies away and the wine oxidizes, these wines turn into amontillado. Oxidative ageing, as the name suggests, is the ageing process where Sherries have no flor in the barrel. The longer a Sherry ages in barrel, the more intense its flavour and the more alcoholic it will become, because as the water in the wine evaporates, the ratio of alcohol to liquid increases.

FINO & MANZANILLA *Say it: fee-no and man-tha-nee-ya*

Both these styles are always completely dry, and are the lightest in alcohol of all Sherries. They're fresh and have a salty, appetite-whetting flavour, so should be drunk fridge-cold. On a hot day, these make an unbeatable zesty aperitif.

AMONTILLADO *Say it: ah-mon-tee-yar-doh*

A step up in richness from fino and manzanilla, this style is usually aged for longer before it's released. It tastes of lightly-toasted nuts and has a tangy orange flavour. Most of it is dry, but some is sweet.

PALO CORTADO *Say it: pah-lo cor-tah-do*

For me, this is the most versatile of Sherry styles. It's a step up in richness from amontillado; in fact, it's often described as having the nose of amontillado and the palate of oloroso. Here, the flavour has caramelized nuts with the freshness of orange and a rich vanilla spice.

OLOROSO *Say it: oll-oh-rosso*

The richest of the dry Sherries, and the one that will have been aged for longest. Oloroso tastes of figs, prunes and liquorice, but it can also be dry or sweet, and both are heavenly.

PEDRO XIMÉNEZ

This is for people with a sweet tooth, is intensely dark in colour and at its best when poured over vanilla ice cream.

MADEIRA

The Portuguese island of Madeira is also the name given to its fortified wine. I think this is the most misunderstood of all fortified wines, yet it's also one of the easiest to understand, because the grape variety dictates the level of sweetness. What's incredible about Madeira is the length of time it can age. These wines can go up to 100 years and still taste amazingly fresh, plus they can last a long time once opened without disappearing – and I'm talking weeks, sometimes months. It's robust but incredibly sensual, all of which makes Madeira ridiculously good value for money.

Sercial

A dry wine with a tangy orange flavour, it has a smoky tobacco taste and good richness, even though it's dry.

Verdelho

As a grape it's the most planted on the island. Off-dry as a wine, it tastes of dried apricots and honey.

Bual/Boal

Medium-sweet as a wine, it's famous for having an incredible perfume of caramel and orange – boiled sweets/hard candy is a common flavour description, and an accurate one.

Malvasia/Malmsey

This is the sweetest Madeira – it's dark brown in colour and tastes of toffee apples, caramelized pineapple and caramelized nuts. Heavenly.

MORE FORTIFIED WINE
VIN DOUX NATUREL

As it translates, this is a 'naturally sweet wine', because of the sugar left in the wine after the fermentation has been stopped. It's a speciality of the south of France, but it's not exclusive to this area. Some of the most common VDNs include Rivesaltes, Muscat, Maury, Banyuls and Samos (see pages 116–121), and smell of orange blossom and have a caramelized orange flavour on the palate – heady stuff. Rivesaltes from France can be white or red, while Muscat de Rivesaltes has a pretty elderflower flavour, but is not as revered as Muscat de Beaumes-de-Venise.

Maurys from French Roussillon are made with Grenache Noir. Although sweet and fortified, these red wines can be rich in tannin so need some time to age and mellow, but they're delicious with chocolate.

Rutherglen in Victoria, Australia, is the most famous fortified wine region in Australia and Muscat is the jewel in its crown. Vines here are extremely old and many date back to the gold rush period of the 1850s. These sweet fortified wines are dark brown in colour and extremely intense after their very long period of ageing in barrels. They often smell and taste of crème brûlée, caramelized nuts, butterscotch, caramel and treacle/molasses.

Sherry

Haven't you heard? Sherry is going through a renaissance. Seriously, it's now the must-have drink in some of the world's coolest cities. The popularity of tapas especially has brought Sherry to the front of the wine list because it has a natural affinity with this style of food. For wine-lovers already wise to Sherry's deliciousness, the whole Sherry scene is extra-exciting at the moment because the bodegas keep coming up with innovative, quirky and limited-edition wines, and these really transport you back to its home in south-west Spain. The renaissance hasn't caught up with everyone just yet, though, and too many Sherry urban myths still exist, so let's tackle these right here, right now.

Urban myth 1: It's all sweet

Forget what's in Grandma's cupboard, a lot of the best Sherry is dry. Like, D-R-Y. In fact, styles like fino and manzanilla are often drier than your average glass of Sauvignon Blanc or Chardonnay.

Urban myth 2: It's all grey and gloopy

Cream Sherry is the thick, sweet Sherry that most people associate with all Sherry, but this is just one style of Sherry, and not the most exciting one, either. Cream Sherry is usually a blend of different sherries that have been deliberately sweetened and coloured. Sherry can range from being clear and pale lemon in colour to light caramel or dark mahogany.

Urban myth 3: It can be made anywhere

Sherry can only be called Sherry if it comes from its designated region in south-west Spain. In other words, there's no such thing as 'Australian Sherry' or 'South African Sherry' or 'French Sherry', etc.

Urban myth 4: It can be kept for years

Please don't keep your Sherry for years. Especially if it's been opened. A fino or manzanilla should be treated like a white wine – keep it for a maximum of two days once opened, preferably in the fridge. The other richer styles shouldn't really be kept for more than a week or two, either.

Urban myth 5: It's too strong

Sherry is a fortified wine, sure, but it can still make some incredibly refreshing wines. The lightest styles, fino and manzanilla, are usually around 15% ABV (alcohol by volume) and taste zingy on the palate. These days you can find many unfortified wines that are just as high in alcohol.

Urban myth 6: It's red

It's a common mistake to make, but it is impossible to make red Sherry – it's only ever made from white grapes.

Urban myth 7: All Sherry is ageless

Most Sherry is given an average age because it's made of a blend of sherries from different years, but you can still find sherries from one year. They are rare and delicious because a bodega will only have released a 'vintage' Sherry if it is a special year.

Urban myth 8: It's only for before dinner

Sherry is one of the most versatile wines around, which means there are styles for before, during and after a meal.

SWEET

When it comes to unfortified sweet wines, classics, like Sauternes, hog the limelight, while German Riesling (unfairly) gets a pretty bad rap. There are actually many styles and grapes used to make sweet wine, although it's true that certain grape varieties lend themselves to making sweet wines better than others. These include Sauvignon Blanc, Muscat, Semillon, Riesling and Gewürztraminer, so you'll see these grapes pop up time and again to make sweet wines all over the word. Often but not always, sweet wines are lower in alcohol, too, because there's too much sugar in the wine for the alcohol fermentation to keep going. They are called many things, including 'dessert wines', although this isn't a favourite of mine as it implies that they're only good for desserts, which isn't true. They're also nicknamed 'sticky wines' and this itself is often shortened to 'stickies'. In the UK, they're often referred to as 'pudding wines', too.

Unfortified sweet wines can be split into four categories, as well as four styles: delicate and floral whites, rich and honeyed whites, sparkling, and red. Below are the most common methods of making sweet wine, and all of them involve having a grape that's high in sugar before the grape juice goes through fermentation to turn into wine.

LATE HARVEST (VENDANGE TARDIVE – VT)
The grapes are deliberately harvested late so the sugar continues to accumulate as the grapes hang on the vine.

BOTRYTIS ('NOBLE ROT')
When grapes are infected with a good rot called *Botrytis cinerea*, they shrivel up as the water evaporates, leaving a high proportion of sugar.

ICEWINE (EISWEIN)
Wine made from grapes that freeze on the vine. When extracting

the juice from the grape, the water is frozen, leaving a high proportion of sugar in the grape.

STRAW WINE
After the grapes are harvested, they're left on mats (often made of straw) to dehydrate, again leaving a high proportion of sugar.

FRANCE
SAUTERNES & BARSAC, BORDEAUX
These are the most famous sweet wines in the world. Sauternes, and within it, Barsac, uses three grapes to make sweet wine: Sauvignon Blanc, Semillon and Muscadelle. They are rich, very honeyed and taste of exotic fruits like mango, but also of orange and nuts. One of the most famous sweet wines in the world is Château d'Yquem, although I like Château Suduiraut, too.

ALSACE
The most common grapes for sweet wine in Alsace are Riesling, Gewurztraminer and Muscat, although these grapes also make excellent dry wines here. Look at the label to tell the difference, if it says 'Vendange Tardive' (VT) or 'Sélection de Grains Nobles' (SGN), the wine will be sweet.

COTEAUX DU LAYON, LOIRE VALLEY
The honeyed white that tastes of candied citrus from this region is underrated and fairly unknown. It's a delicate sweet wine made from Chenin Blanc grapes in the Anjou section of the Loire Valley, where the three most respected sub-regions are Bonnezeaux, Quarts-de-Chaume and Coteaux du Layon.

VOUVRAY, LOIRE VALLEY
Vouvray is in the Touraine part of the Loire Valley, and makes delicate and floral, still or sparkling, as well as dry, off-dry, medium and sweet wines, so it's really worth checking the label properly. The reason the style can vary so much is that the region can't always guarantee its

grapes will be sweet enough to make a full-on sweet wine. Like Coteaux du Layon, Vouvray is made from the Loire's signature white grape, Chenin Blanc.

MONBAZILLAC, SOUTH-WEST FRANCE
Often (and rightly) billed as a wallet-friendly alternative to Sauternes and Barsac, these honeyed whites are made from Sauvignon Blanc, Semillon and Muscadelle.

JURANÇON, SOUTH-WEST FRANCE
These wines, from the Basque corner of France, are a real feather in France's winemaking cap. They fall under two sweetness levels, simply called Jurançon, which is incredibly sweet, or Jurançon Vendange Tardives, which is even sweeter. They are usually made from the Petit Manseng or Gros Manseng grapes, and they taste of caramel, honeysuckle, exotic fruits and vanilla.

PACHERENC DU VIC-BILH, MADIRAN
Dry and sweet white wines made in Madiran have to be called Pacherenc but can drop the du Vic-Bilh. The sweet wines are usually late-harvest wines made from local grapes or Petit Manseng and Petit Courbu.

VIN DE PAILLE, JURA
Jura is France's smallest winemaking region, found east of Burgundy, and its speciality sweet wine is Vin de Paille, a straw wine. Vin de Paille is made from Chardonnay, Savagnin, Poulsard, and sometimes another local grape called Trousseau. It can come in different levels of sweetness, from medium to full-on tooth-tinglingly sweet.

HUNGARY
TOKAJI *Say it: tock-eye*
Hungary's most famous wine and one of the most famous sweet wines in the world. Tokaji the wine comes from Tokaj the region (the 'i' differentiates the wine from the place) and is made mostly with

Furmint grapes, native to Hungary. It's heavenly, rich in caramel, toffee and dried-apricot flavours, and can be expensive.

ITALY

VIN SANTO, TUSCANY

This is a sweet straw wine mainly made from two white grapes: Trebbiano Toscana and Malvasia Bianco. After harvest, the grapes are laid out on mats or hung up to air-dry from the ceiling. They usually have a rich amber colour, which comes from ageing in large wooden barrels, and make a rich and nutty nectar.

MOSCATO D'ASTI, PIEDMONT

Light and fizzy, this pretty Moscato is a useful sweet wine at the end of a meal because it's low in alcohol, around 5.5% ABV (alcohol by volume), and very refreshing, too. Moscato d'Asti often gets confused with the inferior Asti, which is much sweeter and the bubbles are larger so it feels more fizzy.

PASSITO DEL PANTELLERIA, SICILY

Pantelleria is a satellite island off Sicily and *Passito* is the Italian name given to dried-out grapes. Just 50 miles from Tunisia, it's super-hot here. Moscato, is the grape used for this style – it's unctuous and very honeyed.

RECIOTO DELLA VALPOLICELLA & VALPOLICELLA RIPASSO, VENETO

Recioto is a delicious sweet red wine made in Valpolicella. It can be still or slightly sparkling and is made using Corvina, Rondinella and Molinara grapes. Valpolicella Ripasso is the wine made from the dried red grape skins that are used in making the Recioto.

GERMANY

Riesling is king in Germany, as we know. Its sweet wines are usually made from Riesling, following a general hierarchy of sweetness, although if the label says 'Trocken' this is a firm guarantee that the wine is dry.

SPÄTLESE
Translated, this means 'late-picked', but there has been a trend recently to make dry wines with these grapes, even though they are late-picked, so it can be a gamble. Dry or sweet, the wines have a floral, honeyed character.

AUSLESE
Meaning 'select' wines, these grapes hang on the vines until they're deemed sweet enough, so mainly they're late harvest, but sometimes they will have botrytis-affected grapes in them, too. They have a tight acidity and rounded honeyed character.

BEERENAUSLESE (BA) & TROCKENBEERENAUSLESE (TBA)
Made only from botrytis-affected grapes to make Rieslings that are pure and full of life. TBA is a step up in sweetness from BA. It's super-concentrated, super-intense, super-sweet.

EISWEIN (ICEWINE)
Very concentrated, and with such full-on acidity that the wines will age for many years.

AUSTRIA
Austria's sweet-wine hierarchy and vocabulary is influenced by Germany – from Spätlese to Eiswein – but it also has a couple of its own speciality sweet wines. These are also usually made from Riesling.

STROHWEIN, BURGENLAND
As you might have guessed from the name, this is Austria's version of straw wine, and the rules say the grapes must be laid out on straw mats or hung up to air-dry for a minimum of three months to dehydrate. They make honeyed and salty-flavoured sweet wines.

AUSBRUCH, BURGENLAND
Ausbruch is a wine made with botrytis-affected grapes and has a strict

minimum sugar-level stipulation as well as a strict origin. It's a speciality from the town of Rust, and can only come from there.

USA, NEW ZEALAND, AUSTRALIA & CHILE
All of these countries make sweet wines from a variety of grapes. Relaxed winemaking laws mean anything is possible, so they can be made from any grapes in any place, although the most popular ones tend to be made from Semillon, Riesling, Muscat and Sauvignon Blanc.

SOUTH AFRICA
Chenin Blanc is often made into a dessert wine using the straw-wine method here. A few standout producers are Mullineux and De Trafford.

CANADA
Icewine is Canada's speciality, and Riesling is the grape that makes the most exquisite wines, but the Vidal grape is also widely used. This honeyed nectar usually has a fantastic freshness.

Grapes hung to dry for Vin Santo

FIZZ

We sparkling wine drinkers have never had it so good.
While Champagne, Cava and Prosecco is the most
famous fizzy trio around, sparkling wines are made to
a very high standard all over the world these days.
Whether they are dry or sweet, young or old, white,
orange, pink or red, and made in the northern or
southern hemisphere, I'm convinced there's a bottle of
fizz out there to suit every palate, dish and occasion.

THE FIZZ

First, let's get to grips with how the bubbles are locked into wine because it's a pretty major component in what the wine will look like.

TRADITIONAL (CHAMPAGNE) METHOD

This is the most expensive method and it's thought to make the highest-quality sparkling wine, complex enough to age. Here, the second fermentation takes place inside the bottle and the carbon dioxide created by that fermentation dissolves into the wine, making it fizzy. However, the second fermentation isn't just important for the bubbles; it also produces a deposit that's made up of dead yeast cells, called 'lees'.

Traditional-method wines are aged 'on the lees' for a minimum period of time, depending on the style and where it's made. Resting on the lees gives the wine extra flavour and complexity, and can make the wine taste more like bread, which is easy to understand because the lees is yeast. Some regions stipulate this method *must* be used in order for the wine to call itself that particular wine style. These include Cava and Champagne, as well as Franciacorta in Italy, Crémant in France and Methode Cap Classique in South Africa. And although most English sparkling wine is also made this way, there's no requirement that it has to be.

TRANSFER METHOD

This is useful for sparkling wines that are made in large quantities, or wines that will be sold in very large bottles. Here, the wine also goes through a second fermentation in the bottle. After this, it is transferred to a large vat so it can be filtered, then it's rebottled, but there's always the risk that some bubbles get lost between transfers.

TANK (CHARMAT) METHOD

This is good for sparkling wines that are made from aromatic grapes and for early drinking, and that's why it's used for Prosecco, which is made from the floral Glera grape. It involves a second fermentation taking place in a large tank, then transferring the wine into bottles under pressure.

CARBONATION

This method is used for wines that are made for immediate drinking. Here, a still table wine is simply injected with carbon dioxide: a bit like how you would use a Soda Stream.

THE GRAPES

Any grapes can make a sparkling wine. They vary from being very local and relatively unknown to international grapes like Pinot Noir and Chardonnay, which are the two universally admired and thought to make the best sparkling wine. A good number of the best sparkling wines are made from grapes grown in cooler climates, because the natural high acidity in these grapes is the perfect starting point before the wine goes through the enrichening processes involved in making it sparkling.

STYLES, REGIONS & FLAVOURS

BRUT NV

The flagship sparkling wine style. 'Brut' means 'dry' and 'NV' means 'non-vintage', or not from one specific year. Certain producers prefer multi-vintage, where you'll see 'MV' on the label. For this style, older wines will have deliberately been kept in the winery, waiting to be blended. Pulling all these different years together is important, because it ensures the wine tastes the same from year to year – and we wine drinkers have an unspoken deal, we expect a house 'style' that tastes the same, year in, year out.

ROSÉ

The double-whammy of popularity at the moment – sparkling and pink wine – so no wonder sales of pink fizz go from strength to strength. See pages 144–151 to see how fizz is made pink.

BRUT ZERO, BRUT NATURE, ZERO DOSAGE

An intensely dry sparkling wine that's become very popular. The sweetness level of sparkling wine is determined halfway through its production process, when a little topping-up liquid known as *liqueur de tirage* determines how sweet the final wine will be. If you add no sugar to this liqueur de tirage, it falls into the 'Brut Zero' category, which purists love because the wine isn't masked by any sugar.

BLANC DE BLANCS

A fizz made only from white grapes, typically Chardonnay, which is the only main white grape in Champagne, but most places that make a Chardonnay-only sparkling wine will refer to it as a Blanc de Blancs anyway. This is the ultimate crisp and elegant aperitif, but it can age extremely well, too.

BLANC DE NOIRS

A fizz only made from red grapes, which usually means they're made from Pinot Noir or Pinot Meunier, or both. Again, the influence is Champagne. They make fuller sparkling wines than Blanc de Blancs, with more red-fruit richness.

VINTAGE

A sparkling wine from one year. Vintage Champagnes are usually very good value for money, even if they're more expensive than Brut NV. In Champagne, they'll usually only release a vintage if the year is thought to be great. Vintage wines are more common in newer sparkling wine regions because they don't have the bank of older wines in their cellars to make a NV.

PRESTIGE CUVÉE

The crème de la crème, they command high prices. Examples of Champagne prestige cuvées include Cristal, Belle Époque, Comtes de Champagne, R.D., Cuvée Sir Winston Churchill, Krug and Dom Pérignon.

CHAMPAGNE, FRANCE

The benchmark sparkling wine for most people. Champagne is from Champagne, in north-east France; everything made outside of Champagne is sparkling wine. Whatever the style, grape or age of Champagne, it's synonymous with elegance and complexity, because it's fruity but toasty and has many layers of flavour. Champagne is made using the traditional method, and typically from three grapes: Pinot Noir and Pinot Meunier (both red), and Chardonnay (white). It's a great wine to pair with food and can work throughout a meal.

CRÉMANT, FRANCE

Crémant can provide serious value for money and it's the name given to French sparkling wines that aren't from the Champagne region but which are made using the traditional (Champagne) method. They come from many regions and use the local grapes to each area, so they've been practiced to perfection through the generations. With the demand for bubbles increasing and Crémant's affordable prices, we're seeing more and more bottles on the shelves these days.

PROSECCO, ITALY

Prosecco is a region in north-east Italy. Made from the Glera grape in the tank method, it's perky, fruity and still hugely popular.

FRANCIACORTA, ITALY

Italy's equivalent to Champagne is a delicious toasty sparkling wine with serious elegance. Franciacorta is the name of the region and the wine style. Its home is Lombardy, and it is largely made up from Chardonnay and Pinot Nero (Noir), and sometimes Pinot Bianco (Blanc), too. Satèn is a gorgeous Franciacorta style that's silky-smooth in texture, because it has a lower atmospheric pressure than other fizz. Two lovely producers are Fratelli Berlucchi and Bellavista.

METHODE CAP CLASSIQUE, SOUTH AFRICA

The quality sparkling wine from South Africa is often shortened to 'MCC'. Usually made from Sauvignon Blanc, Chenin Blanc, Chardonnay or Pinot Noir, these are flavourful wines made in the traditional method and are improving all the time. Graham Beck and Villiera make good ones.

SPARKLING SHIRAZ, AUSTRALIA
Australian red fizz that is often drunk at Christmas to go with the myriad of flavours on the table (or barbecue). It has the classic juicy black fruit of Shiraz with black pepper, pepped up with bubbles. Seppelt, Peter Lehman and Jacob's Creek all make juicy versions.

TASMANIA, AUSTRALIA
The hub of quality sparkling wine out of Australia, the conditions in Tasmania are cool enough to give the grapes (often Chardonnay and Pinot Noir) the best possible chance of being made into a crisp and fresh sparkling wine. Jansz makes great value-for-money ones.

ENGLAND
In the last decade or so, the English sparkling wine scene has exploded, with new wines and producers popping up all the time, because England has the perfect conditions for Chardonnay and Pinot Noir, the two leading sparkling wine grapes. English fizz has a distinctive apple character. Nyetimber and Ridgeview are the pioneers, but Wiston Estate and Coates & Seely are fabulous, too.

CALIFORNIA, USA
California is making great quality sparkling wine. In fact, there's been a lot of investment from Champagne houses here. These wines are usually made with Pinot Noir and Chardonnay, and are usually very toasty and buttery.

Brazil

This is no new-fangled craze. Brazilian sparkling wine actually celebrated 100 years of production in 2015. As in California, not much is exported, but the quality is improving all the time. Most comes from Serra Gaúcha, its most important winemaking region, found right on the southern tip of the country.

Pupitre Taittinger Champagne cellar, Reims, France

THE BAR

This chapter, essentially, covers how to maximize your enjoyment of wine and it includes just as much everyday stuff – like how to open a bottle of fizz without wasting any when the cork flies across the room, or why wine pros hold the glasses by their stems – as it does wine geekery, like the best temperature to serve different styles. Whatever you use it for, The Bar is here to help you get more out of wine.

TEMPERATURE

SERVING WINE

Although wine pros can get sniffy about the correct serving temperature of their wine, it's not for affectation, because chilling can have many effects on wine, limiting its smells, reducing the sensation of alcohol sweetness, as well as boosting savoury flavours and tannic texture. As a result, the precise temperature to serve a wine is really down to personal preference and how *you* want *your* wine to taste, but that's not to say a few guidelines aren't helpful.

Remember that old-school serving rules — whites should be served from-the-fridge cold, and all reds should be room temperature — are misleading and have changed, because the room temperature advice harks back to the days before central heating, when rooms were generally much cooler than they are today. For more on chilling red wine, see pages 32–33.

More complex wines and ones that are slightly older are generally served a little warmer than young or simple wines, because the extra warmth allows the oxygen to reach the compounds of the wine, causing them to open and release the flavour.

Another way of looking at it is that if you were serving a very budget wine or you feel obliged to drink a guest's wine at dinner but don't like the look of it (let's face it, we've all been there), the best solution is to chill it down because it will mute the flavours.

But if you can't decide on the exact temperature to serve a wine, it's always best to serve it on the side of being too cool rather than too warm, because it's much easier and quicker to warm a wine up than to chill one down.

Despite my saying it's all down to preference, some people still like a bit of guidance, so I've provided some, see page 183. But don't forget: this isn't the be-all-and-end-all; there's definite room for manoeuvre by a couple of degrees here or there. It's not like anyone's going to get

their thermometer out and test that you're getting it right, although there are plenty of temperature gadgets and gizmos to be found (see Resources on page 202) if you really do want to keep track of things.

STORING WINE

This can be as high- or low-maintenance as you choose. If you have expensive wines and want them to last for the longest time possible, it's best NOT to keep them next to an oven, in the garage, in full sunlight, or under strong UV lighting – never buy a dusty bottle behind a shop counter. Each of these things is either responsible for fluctuating conditions or speeding up the ageing process of the wine. Remember, too, that clear glass lets UV rays through more (therefore speeding up its ageing) than brown or green glass.

THE IDEAL CONDITIONS FOR STORING WINE:
• A cool, dark place
• Constant temperature
• 50–60% humidity, to prevent the corks (if the bottles have corks) from drying out
• Bottles on their side, again, to prevent corks from drying out

WINE CABINETS & CHILLERS

Often nicknamed 'fridges', these chillers are the optimum storage solution for those of us who don't have hulking great cellars at home. Specifically designed for wine (as opposed to domestic fridges), they provide all the necessary conditions for storing wine and come in all shapes and sizes, so they can fit into whatever space you have available. Liebherr, EuroCave and Caple are three good brands.

WINE STYLE	TEMPERATURE
Sparkling	5-8°C (40-45°F)
Aromatic, simple, light white	8°C (45°F)
White	10°C (50°F)
Rich, mature white or orange	12°C (54°F)
Rosé	8-10°C (45-50°F)
Aromatic, simple, light red	12°C (54°F)
Red	14°C (57°F)
Rich, mature red	16°C (60°F)
Light, floral sweet	8°C (45°F)
Rich, honeyed sweet	11°C (52°F)
Fortified	Varies with age and sweetness level

WINE PROPS

OPENING

THE FOIL

Cutting the foil can be as simple as you want it to be. If you're in a hurry, most corkscrews will just pierce the foil and the cork will pull through it, but that leaves rough and jagged edges. The most common way of trimming the foil is using a foil cutter, which is a little horseshoe-shaped device that is widely available.

To remove the foil, place the cutter over the top of the bottle and twist it back and forth – the foil head should cut off cleanly.

Some foil cutters, however, only cut the foil at the top of the lip that you'll find on most wine bottlenecks. In the wine trade, the common place to cut the foil is at the bottom of this lip, which is often achieved by using the little knife on foldaway corkscrews.

REMOVING CORKS

Corkscrews come in all shapes, sizes and brands these days, so it's down to our choice of style, price and functionality. The two most popular are the lever model and the foldaway Waiter's Friend®.

The lever model is popular and fast, but not a space-saver. The enormous levers of this corkscrew clasp the top of the wine bottle and pull the cork through with hardly any effort at all. Then you reverse the pulling action to remove the cork from the device. It works brilliantly with natural corks, but I've had many sticky moments trying to remove plastic corks from one of these.

A Waiter's Friend® is cheaper, and the most common. As the name suggests, it's a foldaway corkscrew that's widely used in the wine and restaurant trade. It's strong, durable and doesn't need much effort. Plus, it has a little knife to cut the foil as well as a crown cap bottle opener.

CORK RETRIEVER

This is a little prong-like device aimed at rescuing parts of a cork that have broken off mid-opening. It's not a necessity by any means, but could be useful, especially if you have a collection of older wines.

OPENING SPARKLING WINE

If a sparkling wine isn't chilled enough or it's been shaken before opening, it will be noisy and messy to open. For a seamless, quiet opening, remove the foil – usually there's a little tab on the foil to help – untwist and loosen the wire cage that covers the cork, then firmly grab the top of the bottle with your writing hand, the base of the bottle with the other, and slowly twist your hands in different directions until you feel the cork loosen. It might not come naturally at first, but practice definitely makes perfect with this.

BEFORE SERVING

DECANTING

Like with corkscrews, decanters also come in all shapes, sizes and brands, and although you can get something imposing and impressive, a lot of decanting is done for practical rather than aesthetic reasons. There's no right or wrong here, but if you have specific requirements, then buy your decanter from a glassware specialist and ask for advice.

Complex wines, whether they're sparkling, white, red, sweet or fortified, benefit from decanting, because the process involves exposing the wine to the air, and contact with oxygen releases a wine's aroma. I say 'complex' wines, because wines that are light in character just won't improve in a decanter – they have nothing more to give.

If you're decanting to catch sediment – which will rule out most white and sparkling wines – the best method is to lay a piece of muslin/cheesecloth over the top of the decanter and pour the wine through the material. If you find muslin/cheesecloth hard to come by, there are alternatives you can use. I often use a tea-leaf strainer, while low-denier tights/stockings can also work as a decanting mesh.

There are no strict rules as to how long you decant the wine before it's served, and it can depend on the temperature you want the wine to be served at. However, if a wine is very old (to the point of being fragile – I'm talking about, say, a 50-year-old red Burgundy), then it needs to be decanted and served almost immediately rather than left to sit in a decanter for an hour or more. This kind of wine would be so delicate its aroma and flavour could get totally lost if left sitting around in a decanter for too long, so take care.

CLEANING DECANTERS

The nooks and crannies inside a decanter can be a nightmare to clean and dry, but there are a few neat little inventions that can help. These include specialist glass brushes, cleaning fluids and metal cleaning balls.

I'm a big fan of drying crystals: silica crystals are held within what looks like a fabric snake that absorbs any moisture inside the decanter.

It's also useful to swill your decanter with a little water or wine each time before you fill it up again, discarding the water or wine, to remove any impurities.

AFTER IT'S BEEN OPENED

There are loads of ways we can attempt to keep a wine going (to stop it from oxidizing). The most basic way is to re-cork and chill it in the fridge. It's not useless, but it's cheap and the least effective. A more technical option is to spray argon gas (available in a tube like a hairspray cannister) into the bottle. This inert and odourless gas is heavier than air and when sprayed across the surface of the wine, it prevents oxidization.

The Coravin™ system has been around for a few years now. It's a device that's still work-in-progress, but fantastic for sampling older, rarer wines without wasting them. A needle is inserted into the cork to extract the wine, and as the needle enters, the bottle is pressurized with argon gas that forces the wine up through the needle and into a glass.

GLASSWARE

If the wine you drink says something about you, then so too does your choice of wine glass. They come in all shapes, sizes, colours and costs, and while most serious wine glasses are clear, some also now come in black to remove the potential for any prejudice by a professional taster (many of whom will refer to glasses as 'stemware', or 'stems').

If you mean business with wine, even if you're still a beginner, I'd spend as much as you can on a wine glass, because the quality of the tasting experience – in other words, your perception of the wine – really improves with a good-quality glass. I'm pretty relaxed about my choice of glass in general, but, I have to confess I have one go-to favourite and one personal nemesis.

MY GO-TO FAVOURITE

A few years ago, I discovered a weightless glass that could be washed in the dishwasher. In fact, the manufacturer recommends that it should be washed in the dishwasher. Sound too good to be true? Well, it works. This is the Universal glass made by a manufacturer called Zalto, and it's perfect for my daily professional use. Made from titanium crystal (see below) for extra strength, I was astonished when I was first shown this glass as someone just dropped it on the floor and it didn't smash. Incredible.

Lead crystal versus titanium crystal

Manufacturers have started making wine glasses using titanium crystal instead of lead crystal. By replacing the lead oxide with titanium oxide, glasses can't stain or be easily scratched, and are very, very strong.

Whether you wash your glasses by hand or in the dishwasher, it's always good to rinse them with water or wine before you fill them up. This will get rid of any cleaning product residue, which can seriously affect a wine's performance, dumbing down flavour and aroma, and making sparkling wines go flat.

ONE TO AVOID

I could de-snob myself about this if I really wanted to, but there is one glass that I really can't stand, and as much as I love most things with retro-cool cachet, I draw the line at the infamous Paris Goblet. Once a staple wine glass for bistros and public houses, they've slowly been phased out, and I'm not surprised. They look ugly, are impractical (just try swirling a decent glass of wine around without some sloshing over the side) and they don't hold much wine.

SHAPE & SIZE

If you're interested in fashion over function, this bit isn't for you. But if you're looking for a wine glass that gets the most out of the wine within it, then it could be worth looking at manufacturers which have different glass shapes for different grape varieties and styles. The pioneer of this revolutionary idea was Claus Riedel, who started making wine glasses this way more than 50 years ago, and the Riedel range is still going strong today (see Resources on page 202). If you only have the budget and space for a few glasses, try to get different ones for sparkling, white, red and fortified wines at least.

RED Usually served with larger bowls because they allow the aromas and flavours of the wine to open out, much in the same way decanting does (see pages 185–186).

WHITE Served in narrower glasses than for red wine, to capture white wine's fresh, fruity flavours.

SPARKLING Traditionally tall and thin, this shape makes the most of the energetic bubbles shooting to the top, but the flute has now started to widen.

FORTIFIED A smaller glass is best, just to emphasize the fruit flavours rather than the higher alcohol. A small version of a white wine glass could do the job.

TRENDS IN GLASSWARE

It might sound a bit crazy but, just as there are trends with wine, there are trends with wine glasses, too.

CHAMPAGNE & FIZZ

Champagne and other high-calibre fizz are increasingly served in wider glasses rather than the classic tall flutes. Even though the narrow flute channels bubbles to the top of the glass, it doesn't make the most of the complexity of these wines. They deserve to open out a bit so you can really enjoy their flavour, which means they need a wider bowl. Many bars and restaurants now use a compromised version; the glass is noticeably taller and thinner than your average wine glass, but it has a wider bowl than it used to, to show off the wine's complexity.

TUMBLERS

'What?' I hear you say. Well, tapas bars and modern restaurants often now serve still wine in little glass tumblers. I really like this rebellious take on serving wine because it removes the snobbery and pretension from drinking wine. The only downside is that you can't swirl the wine around for a good sniff.

Same wine, different glass

I've been sceptical about these experiments in the past. Ones that are done with the same wine and different glasses, even though the conclusion is usually the same – that the shape and material of the 'glass' DOES affect how a wine tastes. So, I conducted a little experiment in my kitchen and it really hit home just how differently a wine can behave and taste when drunk from different vessels. Here are the results.

The experiment

I used a Premier Cru Brut NV Champagne, made from 50% Chardonnay and equal parts Pinot Noir and Pinot Meunier, and seven different containers to drink it from. I especially wanted to use a sparkling wine, because I also wanted to see whether the 'glasses' changed the effect of the bubbles. And, just to be fair, I rinsed each glass out with some of the Champagne before using it. I've listed them in order of success, just to give you an idea of how each one performed.

1 CHAMPAGNE FLUTE

No surprises here. This flute was a modern one, so it had a relatively wide bowl, rather than being a tall and thin column-shaped flute, and the Champagne tasted best from it. The wine had a strong aroma – it smelt of lemon cheesecake (citrus and biscuit/cookie) – and the bubbles in the mouth were energetic and precise.

2 SHERRY COPITA

The most similar in shape to the flute, and although the wine wasn't as aromatic, the aromas were still very obvious, albeit with a heavier and richer biscuit/cookie character. Again, in the mouth, the flavour was rich and intense, with that toasty, biscuit/cookie flavour really showing through, plus the bubbles stayed neat and precise rather than foaming up.

3 CERAMIC MUG

Surprised this is third place? I was. This showed a good, toasty Champagne aroma, the fizz was energetic but not foamy, and the flavour was rich.

4 LARGE RED WINE GLASS

The Champagne showed barely any aroma but if you sniffed very hard, it smelt a little bit toasty. The rim had the same effect on the fizz as the glass tumbler (below), it was mega-foamy, so much so it was hard to control in the mouth.

5 GLASS TUMBLER

I could barely smell anything with this. The wide rim of the tumbler really made the bubbles froth up in the mouth, although I could taste some lemon flavours.

6 CHILD'S PLASTIC BEAKER

Completely dead on the nose. Nothing at all. The bubbles were energetic without being foamy but the flavour of the wine was metallic and unpleasant. Definitely not recommended.

7 DISPOSABLE WHITE PLASTIC BEAKER

I gave a deserved no score for this. The wine had no aroma, the bubbles disappeared instantly and there was no flavour.

WINE STYLES & FOOD MATCHING
RED & ROSÉ

RED

LIGHT

Dolcetto & Barbera ➜ cherry · spice

Cabernet Franc ➜ rhubarb · herbaceous

Pinot Noir & Gamay ➜ raspberry · strawberry

charcuterie
fish
lamb
pasta
pizza

MEDIUM

Syrah/Shiraz ➜ black pepper · blackberry

Merlot ➜ plum · beetroot/beet

Sangiovese ➜ cherry · raspberry · mushroom

Carmenère ➜ chocolate · spice

Blaufränkisch ➜ cherry · beetroot/beet

Grenache ➜ plum · blackcurrant

Montepulciano ➜ cherry · black tea

beef
cured pork
game
lamb
spicy food

BOLD

Cabernet Sauvignon ➜ blackcurrant · mint

Tempranillo ➜ meaty · leather

Nebbiolo ➜ black pepper · cherry · mushroom

Malbec ➜ blackcurrant · smoky

Zinfandel ➜ chocolate · liquorice

Pinotage ➜ smoky · coffee

Touriga Nacional ➜ blackcurrant · fruit cake

Tannat ➜ oaky · spice

beef
game
mushroom

Whether you know the grape you want, the flavour you are in the mood for, or the food you're eating, we all need a little shortcut at some point in our lives, so here's a quick reference guide for those moments.

ROSÉ

LIGHT

Pinot Noir ➜ strawberry · raspberry

Cabernet Franc ➜ cherry · herbaceous

Merlot ➜ cranberry · strawberry

Grenache ➜ strawberry · pomegranate

cheese
fish
salads
vegetables

MEDIUM-BODIED

Syrah/Shiraz ➜ cherry · spice

Cabernet Sauvignon ➜ raspberry · black pepper

Grenache, non-French ➜ strawberry · cream

Touriga Nacional ➜ pomegranate · grapefruit

Negroamaro ➜ cherry · spice

Malbec ➜ pomegranate · strawberry

barbecues
fish
picnics
spicy food

OFF-DRY

White Zinfandel ➜ strawberry · cream

White Merlot ➜ strawberry · cream

aperitif
dessert

WINE STYLES & FOOD MATCHING
WHITE

AROMATIC

Pinot Grigio → pear · elderflower

Albariño → floral · salty · zesty

Dry Muscat → grape

Dry (young) Riesling → lime · ginger

Gewürztraminer → rose petal · ginger

Torrontés → rose petal · citrus peel

}

fish
salads
spicy food
vegetables

BOLD

Oaked Chardonnay → buttery · honey · mushroom

Oaked Chenin Blanc → waxy · creamy · mushroom

Oaked Viura (white Rioja) → smoky · vanilla · mushroom

}

pork
poultry
mushroom

MEDIUM-BODIED

Sauvignon Blanc → herbaceous · passion fruit
Unoaked Chardonnay → melon · apple
Grüner Veltliner → herbaceous · citrus

> barbecues
> fish
> picnics
> spicy food

Viognier → peach · apricot
Unoaked Chenin Blanc → nuts · grapefruit
Semillon → apple · nuts
Godello → peach
Pinot Gris → waxy · orange
Older Riesling → nuts · waxy

> chicken
> pork
> poultry
> spicy food

WINE STYLES & FOOD MATCHING
FORTIFIED, SWEET & FIZZ

FORTIFIED

Younger Sherry & younger Madeira → salty · citrus ⎫ game
Older Sherry & older Madeira → caramel · nuts ⎬ spicy food
⎭ tapas

Pedro Ximénez Sherry → liquorice · prune ⎫
Red Port → fruit cake · fig ⎪
Tawny Port → dried fruit · toffee ⎪ aperitif
White Port → citrus · herbaceous ⎬ chocolate
Marsala → fig · nuts ⎪ dessert
Rutherglen Muscat → prune · leather ⎭

SWEET

Moscato d'Asti ➔ floral · grape — } aperitif

Vouvray & Auslese ➔ honey · peach — } spicy food

Vendage Tardive (VT) 'Late Harvest' ➔ honey

Sauternes, Monbazillac, Sélection de Grains Nobles (SGN), Icewine ➔ honey · mango

Beerenauslese (BA) & Trockenbeerenauslese (TBA) ➔ honey · peach

Tokaji & Vin Santo ➔ caramel · orange · nuts

Vin de Paille 'Straw Wine' ➔ nuts · salty

} cheese dessert

FIZZ

Champagne ➔ toasty · citrus

Franciacorta, Crémant,

Methode Cap Classique, Cava ➔ creamy · nuts

English sparkling wine ➔ apple · nuts

} cheese fried food poultry

Prosecco ➔ floral · pear — } aperitif fish salads

Syrah/Shiraz ➔ blackcurrant · black pepper — } beef

Brachetto ➔ cherry · raspberry — } chocolate

Party wines

It doesn't matter how much you like it, it's always a risk cracking open a quirky, off-beat wine at a party. The most successful party wines are well known and classic, because it's much better to have people actually drink the wine than be left with cases of the stuff afterwards. So yes, crowd-pleasing, well-known classics are the way to go, and the ones that usually work best are the ones that shout 'LOOK AT ME!' when they're in the glass and in the mouth. In other words, obvious wines, not wimpy wines – and if possible, ones that are going to match a range of food, too.

Should I serve fizz?

Some people demand it, some people expect it, and even if they weren't expecting it and are greeted with a glass, everyone at a party loves fizz. Champagne is the ultimate in luxury, so if the budget stretches that far, it's a crowd-pleasing no-brainer. Although Prosecco is easier on the party budget, there's a lot of value to be had with Crémant, which is French – so many people will assume it's a Champagne anyway. It's made in the same way as Champagne, so it has class, but can come in at half the price or better.

Which white?

Sauvignon Blanc is one of the most identifiable wine flavours in the world. It can smell and taste of anything from freshly mown grass to green vegetables and from citrus to exotic fruit. But the point here is that its flavour is loved by many, known by many and it can match many foods. Plus, a decent one doesn't cost the earth.

Which rosé?

A dry rosé is a great party wine. It's very versatile with food and it looks attractive, especially if you have a deeply coloured one, which is easy enough to find if you buy one from the New World, Spain or Portugal, or if it's made from Syrah/Shiraz or Cabernet Sauvignon.

Which red?

BEAUJOLAIS Bursting with juicy red fruits and full of life, a young and bouncy Beaujolais is great with all sorts of food. If you want the richest type of Beaujolais to match, say, red meat, or you have a decent budget, get a Cru, like Morgon; if you want something cheaper, the next step down – but still a delicious and friendly version – would say 'Beaujolais-Villages' on the label.

SYRAH/SHIRAZ It's hard to beat a robust red like Syrah/ Shiraz. Not only do you get decent bang for your buck, it packs in plenty of flavour, and in summer, it's the perfect match for a barbecue.

Are there other ways to serve wine?

PINK PORT CRUSH (SUMMER COCKTAIL) Pink Port makes a brilliant base for a summery, fresh cocktail. Use it as a base, then top it up with elderflower cordial and tonic water, with loads of ice and quartered strawberries to garnish. It's the ultimate refreshing summer drink.

MULLED PALO CORTADO (WINTER COCKTAIL) My take on the standard mulled wine is a gorgeous winter-warming alternative. Pour a bottle of dry palo cortado into a saucepan or pot set over a gentle heat. Add 40 ml/1½ oz. of ginger liqueur, 4 dried figs, 3 whole cloves, 4 teaspoons of clear honey, the grated zest of 1 orange, 1 cinnamon stick and 1 whole nutmeg, grated. Warm until hot, without boiling, then strain and serve.

RESOURCES

BOOKS

Niki Segnit
The Flavour Thesaurus
(Bloomsbury, 2010)

Jancis Robinson, Julia
Harding and José
Vouillamoz
Wine Grapes
(Allen Lane, 2012)

Hugh Johnson and
Jancis Robinson
*The World Atlas of
Wine*
(Mitchell Beazley, 2013)

Tom Stevenson and
Essi Avellan
*World Encyclopedia of
Champagne &
Sparkling Wine*
(Absolute Press, 2013)

Jancis Robinson
*The Oxford Companion
to Wine*
(Oxford University
Press, 2006)

ONLINE

Liv-ex
www.liv-ex.com
An invaluable source of
information if you're
interested in wine
investment.

Vinography
www.vinography.com
A useful and
informative North
American-based blog.

The Wine Gang
www.thewinegang.com
(but, of course!)
To find out which wines
to buy in the UK.

Wine-Searcher and
The Wine Web
www.wine-searcher.
com
www.wineweb.com
To track down where a
wine is sold.

MAGAZINES

Decanter
www.decanter.com
A UK-based consumer
wine magazine's site
with tips, news and
regional reports.

World of Fine Wine
www.worldoffinewine.
com
A UK-based wine
magazine's site with
in-depth and cerebral
wine articles.

Wine Enthusiast
www.winemag.com

A USA-based wine
magazine with reviews,
news and recipes, too.

RETAILERS

Berry Bros. & Rudd
www.bbr.com
A great wine merchant
in the UK with a
website packed with
information.

EuroCave
www.eurocave.co.uk
A UK-based one-stop
shop for glasses,
decanters, wine chillers
and all kinds of wine
paraphernalia.

The Wine Society
www.thewinesociety.
com
A great wine merchant
in the UK with a
website packed with
information.

INDEX

PICTURE CREDITS

All photography by Toby Scott except:
Page 25 Per Karlsson, BKWine 2/Alamy Stock Photo; p31 Vittoria/Alamy Stock Photo; p40l Pakin Songmor/Getty Images; p40r John Harper/Getty Images; p47 Ivoha/Alamy Stock Photo; p52 ErnestoGravelpond/Alamy Stock Photo; p5c Joan Ransley/Getty Images; p63 Chantal Seigneurgens/Getty Images; p75 Stephen Hughes/Alamy Stock Photo; p103 Chris Mellor/Alamy Stock Photo; p109 Photobyte/Alamy Stock Photo; p115 Julian Eales/Alamy Stock Photo; p121 Garden Photo World/Georgianna Lane/Getty Images; p127 Ariane Lohmar/Getty Images; p133 Ian Shaw/Alamy Stock Photo; p137 Chris Brignell/Alamy Stock Photo; p151 Paul Atkinson/Getty Images; p169 Bon Appetit/Alamy Stock Photo; p177 John Kellerman/Alamy Stock Photo.

ACKNOWLEDGMENTS

A huge, gigantic, colossal thanks to all these wonderful people, all of whom have helped more than they probably know (and some of whom will sadly never know): Mum and Dad, Jane Carr, Johnny Ray, Anne Kibel, Amelia and Matthew Jukes, Elizabeth Ferguson, Will Drew, Jancis Robinson, Michael Cox, Fiona Beckett, Charlotte Hey, Mary Rochester Gearing, Helen Chesshire, Hannah Tovey, Chris, Anne and Philip Parkinson, Astrid Lewis, Simon McMurtrie, Graham Holter, Patrick Schmitt, Patrick Sandeman, Andy Clarke, Bruno Cernecca, Hugh Johnson, Charles Metcalfe, Janan Ganesh, Anne Scott, Robert Joseph, Gary Simons, Stefan Chomka, Ewan Lacey, Kathrin Leaver, Amy Grier, James Winter, Lisa Smosarski, Steve Grimley, Gary Werner, the rest of The Wine Gang – Tom Cannavan, Joanna Simon, Anthony Rose and David Williams, everyone at Ryland Peters & Small, including Manisha Patel and especially Stephanie Milner, and finally, my university tutor who told me to do my dissertation on wine.

ABOUT THE AUTHOR

© John Moore

Jane Parkinson is an award-winning wine writer. She's a wine expert on Saturday Kitchen (BBC 1), Wine Editor for *Restaurant* magazine and recommends wines with recipes in *Stylist*. Jane also contributes to a range of publications including *Square Meal* and *Decanter* and is often heard voicing her opinion in newspapers, on television and radio. She is one of five members of The Wine Gang, an independent group of wine specialists, and is a regular presenter at events and fairs such as the BBC GoodFood Show. She lives in London, grew up in South Wales and loves to explore the wine-producing regions of the world. She was the winner of the Chairman's Award at the Louis Roederer International Wine Writers' Awards 2009 and the Communicator of the Year Award at the International Wine & Spirit Competition 2014.